M000223615

THE C...
HARDLY LUMBER
COMPANY

and other tales of
growing up in
northern Michigan

**a collection of stories
written and compiled by**

E. Dan Stevens

© 2018 E. Dan Stevens

All Rights Reserved.

No part of this publication may be reproduced, stored in a retrieval system, or transmitted, in
any form or by any means, electronic, mechanical, photocopying, recording, or otherwise,
without the written permission of the author.

First published by Dog Ear Publishing
4011 Vincennes Rd
Indianapolis, IN 46268
www.dogearpublishing.net

ISBN: 978-1-4575-6103-0

This book is printed on acid-free paper.

Printed in the United States of America

TABLE OF CONTENTS

PART II - Stories by Contributors

PART III - Stories by Ross O. Stevens

INTRODUCTION

June 6, 1952, was the day my new life began. On that day, only a month and a few days after my ninth birthday, I, along with parents, three older siblings and collie dog, Duchess, arrived in Atlanta, Michigan, population 300. We had all been stuffed into our family car, a 1950 blue Chevrolet Deluxe, for the three days it had taken us to travel from Raleigh, North Carolina, to our new hometown in northeastern Michigan.

For my dad, a former professor at North Carolina State College (now University), it was an opportunity to return to the place of his birth and childhood and the pursuits of his father, farming and lumbering.

For my North Carolina born and raised mother and for my older brother and sisters, Atlanta and Montmorency County, Michigan, were settings for varying chapters of their lives. For me, much like Dad, this small county in the most sparsely populated area of Michigan's Lower Peninsula has been my home base from that day onward.

Following my retirement from full-time professional activities in 2003, I began chronicling some of my memories of places and events from my growing-up years for publication in the Montmorency County Tribune. This volume comprises those tales from over the years, plus seven written by my father during the 60s, plus nine others that were written by other writers with interesting experiences to share.

I am publishing these stories and vignettes primarily to preserve a few memories and a little of Montmorency County history. If the reader gets a laugh or two from some of the stories, I'll consider it a plus.

Dan Stevens

PART I

THE CAN'T HARDLY LUMBER COMPANY

By E. Dan Stevens (2006)

Larry wasn't laughing. But I was, almost hysterically, and so was Darrell. Even Bob Teets started to chuckle a little, a far cry from his frantic shouting of only seconds before, "Dan, Darrell - come quick. Larry's pinned under the tractor!"

Darrell and I were a couple of hundred yards away from the old railroad grade when we heard Bob calling. Darrell was hacking limbs off a downed tree with an axe, and I was sharpening our chain saw when it happened. "...pinned under the tractor!" We both started running, picturing Larry under the weight of an overturned tractor.

The four of us, Bob Teets, Larry Wilson, Darrell Briley and I, spent the summer of 1960 cutting and hauling pulpwood from a stand of poplar trees on my dad's farm in Hillman Township. Darrell had just graduated from Atlanta High School. Larry and I were between our junior and senior years, and Bob would be a junior when we went back in the fall. We called ourselves the Can't Hardly Lumber Company. It was a fitting name.

My dad was running for his first term in the Michigan House of Representatives that year and wasn't operating his sawmill where I had worked in summers past. He gave us the poplar trees and provided us with equipment, mostly I guess, to keep us out of trouble for the summer.

In addition to a Homelite chain saw, he let us use an old Ferguson tractor and a two-wheeled trailer to haul the pulpwood logs to a road where they could be picked up by a truck. The tractor had rubber front wheels, but the rear wheels were steel with four-inch lugs for traction. It ran pretty well, but sometimes the clutch stuck. It wouldn't always disengage straightaway when the pedal was pushed.

Larry and Bob had just hauled a load of logs to the main pile. After unloading the trailer, Larry got on the tractor to turn it around on the old railroad grade that served as the road to our log pile. After swinging the tractor and trailer around at a wide area along the grade, he pushed the clutch to stop the tractor. Nothing happened. The tractor kept going - right over the side of the grade and down a fifteen foot high embankment.

"Larry tried to jump, but the brake pedal caught his right foot," Bob explained later. "Somehow he ended up under the tractor as it rolled down the bank. He was rolling along the ground between the front wheels and the back wheels. He was just staying ahead of those steel lugs. Then he rolled up against that small log and stopped."

When Darrell and I reached the grade, we could see that the tractor's left rear wheel had stopped when it hit the log. Larry lay face down between the right rear wheel and the log. The tractor was stalled. We heard words coming from Larry's mouth that even a seasoned lumberjack would be proud of. That's when we knew he was okay.

I guess it was the relief to find that he wasn't squashed - as we had imagined - that made us start laughing, but it was also sort of funny, him lying there not able to move and swearing. One of those four-inch steel lugs had gone between his legs. Another inch or two from where it stopped when the tractor stalled, and well, I don't think his two wonderful children would have happened later on in his life.

Of course we couldn't laugh forever. He was still pinned between the log and the steel tractor wheel. We decided to block the front wheels to keep the tractor from going any further down the bank. We then carefully worked the log away from where Larry was lying. Relief was evident all around when the tractor stayed put while Larry had enough room to slide out from under that wheel. He lost some skin on his back, I think from hitting the log as he rolled down the grade, but was otherwise unhurt.

After he crawled free, Larry looked at Bob and said, "You really didn't have to tell me not to go anywhere while you went to get those guys."

That was Larry's last day with the Can't Hardly Lumber Company. Bob, Darrell and I gave it another week. Darrell left for the Navy soon after and the rest of us had to start football practice.

The little money we made that summer is long gone, but we've managed to save a few of our stories.

PIRATES OF THE THUNDER BAY

By E. Dan Stevens (2006)

It must have been the pirate movie they showed at the V.F.W. Hall that summer that led to the Atlanta river war of 1952. I remember we all liked that picture show so much that most of us went back to see it again on the second night.

There were at least two different movies each week shown at the V.F.W. Hall during the early 50's. The projectors were upstairs in the east part of the building (now the State Police office) and the screen was along the west wall of the old gymnasium (which collapsed under a snow load some years later.) Patrons sat in seats placed on the gym floor. It was a great service to the community provided by the returned veterans of World War II.

I was nine in 1952. It was the year most of the side streets were paved in Atlanta, Michigan. It was also the year of the Great River War. It wasn't a real war because our opponents were also our friends. It was more like a game. We fought with wooden sticks (our swords), and from canoes and duck boats (our pirate ships), and we strictly followed our rules of battle. Get touched by an opponent's "sword" and you were "dead" for the rest of the battle. It was the north side of the river against the south.

Kim Bleech told me that he and Terry Brooks collected survey stakes from an abandoned roadway project south of town. These were used by both sides as our swords. Most of us carved a handle on one end to fit our hand, but otherwise our respective weapons were the same.

We ranged in age from eight or nine to twelve or thirteen. I can't remember all who participated, but the south-side leader was Ben Thompson.

I was a traitor, I guess, because we lived that summer in Charley and Stella Brown's farmhouse, south of the river, but I was in the northside "gang." Our leaders were Dennis Briley and Terry Brooks. We were "headquartered" at the fort behind Dennis' house on the river, just west of the present Northwoods Gallery.

There were a number of skirmishes out on the river that summer. One or two duck boats (usually homemade) or canoes from each side would meet in the middle of the river and our stick-swords would fly until all in one boat or the other had been "killed." Sometimes one or more of us might jump overboard and swim for shore to avoid being touched by an opponent's sword. That tactic wasn't always successful. Our foes could usually paddle faster than we could swim.

The Great River War climaxed when the southsiders raided our stronghold, the Briley Fort. The fort was built around the land side of a small point projecting into the river behind Darrell and Dennis Briley's house. For a bunch or kids' work, it was pretty well constructed. Its walls were made of pine logs, placed vertically along the base of the point. It even had a catwalk. The wall protected us from the land side, but we had no shield from the river.

I think the big battle was in late August, just before school started. We must have had some pre-arrangement because eight or ten of us were assembled to defend the fort early that afternoon. We closed the wooden gate and readied our swords. Dennis and Terry directed each of us to defend a portion of the fort wall. They would protect the side fronting the river-.

We didn't have to wait long. A raiding party of six, or so, southsiders could be seen approaching the fort from the east, coming along a path from the back of the V.F.W. Hall. Their initial attempt to force open the gate failed and a couple of them were "killed" trying to scale the fort's wall. We were beginning to feel confident that we could defend the fort.

Alas, just as the raiding party was storming the gate a second time, we turned to find that two duck boats had just landed at the riverbank inside the fort. Ben Thompson and Kim Bleech, two of their best (older) fighters and a couple of others scrambled ashore. One of them managed to unlock the gate before we could stop him.

From then on it was a wild affair as the remaining raiders rushed through the gateway. For a while we gave as good as we got, with many on both sides dropping from a sword's touch. I was an early casualty following the marine landing. I remember that Austin Briley from the south side, another early victim, and I sat on a willow trunk watching those still standing go at each other with their wooden swords.

It wasn't long before most of the swashbucklers from both sides had fallen. At the end there were only two left, Darrell Briley from our side and Ben Thompson from theirs. It was a physical mismatch. Darrell was ten and Ben was twelve or thirteen.

I would like to say that it had a David and Goliath ending, but such was not to be. Darrell jumped up on the catwalk and ran to the west end of the fort wall where a large willow tree grew alongside. He managed to evade Ben for a few seconds by ducking behind one willow tree and then another, but it was only a matter of time before Ben guessed right and caught Darrell between two branches. The battle was over. The south-siders had captured our fort.

For the next hour or so, all of us from both sides relived the combat. Those of us who were out early had little to say except to temper the claims of some of our more successful comrades when they became too exaggerated. But we all had fun.

The war didn't carry over to the next summer that I remember, maybe because the V.F.W. didn't show any more pirate movies. It is somewhat painful still for me to admit that the pirate gang from the south side of the river has never since been dethroned.

TROUT FISHING WITH TUFFY

By E. Dan Stevens (2006)

I learned lots of things from Tuffy while I was growing up in Atlanta, Michigan, but of all that he taught me I treasure trout fishing the most. I was nine or ten and he was eleven or twelve the first time we went. Barger Creek. It was a day I'll never forget.

If you are between 55 and 85 and lived anywhere in Montmorency County during the 50's, 60's, 70's or 80's, you know who Tuffy was. For the rest of you, he was Tuffy Marlatt. His nickname was somewhat misleading. Oh, he was tough enough, and I was always glad to be on his side, but he was a genuinely nice person throughout his life. Only his mother, Irene, called him by his given name, Lawrence. Some of his brothers used his middle name, Jesse. It was a chilly June morning. My dad dropped me at the Marlatt farm, just west of the Big Rock store, on his way to work. I was in time for breakfast, I remember. It was Wheaties and milk direct from their cows.

After breakfast, Tuffy "borrowed" some cat-gut line, a half-dozen small hooks and two spinners from his dad's tackle box, and we were off. I was wearing his coat, and he was wearing one of his father's Mackinaw jackets. It was only a little too big. The fishing line and hooks were in the breast pocket of the Mackinaw. We weren't carrying any poles, but Tuffy had a large jackknife in his pants pocket. He had dug some worms before I arrived. We took turns carrying them in an old coffee can.

Barger Creek is not very large. In most places we could jump across. It starts at what was then called Spiess Lake (before it was dammed to form what is now called Lake Inez) and empties into the Thunder Bay River a ways upstream from the Ford Bridge. We walked down the highway to the Big Rock store, and then south on the dirt road to the creek. We followed the creek downstream to a place where it entered a cedar swamp.

There, Tuffy stopped and cut our poles from saplings along the bank, each about six feet long, and he tied on the line. He first carved away the bark from the end where the line would be wound. The line could be lengthened or shortened by rotating the pole. He also showed me how to tie on a spinner with a hook attached. We were ready to fish.

First, though, I needed to know some things. "Trout are spooked by anything," he told me. "A shadow, a vibration in the ground, something knocked in the water. Anything like that and we can forget about that trout hole. So walk softly as far away from the creek as you can and sneak up on the hole. Get just close enough to stick your pole out and let the line down into the water."

Most of the "holes" were under old moss-covered cedar trunks lying across the creek. He showed me how to let the line drop in above the trunk and be carried by the current into the hole. Sure enough, we soon started catching brook trout. Size, however, was another issue.

The legal size for brook trout in those days was seven inches. We had neglected to bring any kind of ruler or other measuring device, so we were unable to tell exactly which fish were legal and which were not. It didn't really matter, though. Tuffy had his own standard. It was either an "eater" or not. If he thought it was big enough to eat we kept it.

We for sure threw back the three and four-inchers. Above that I cannot say for certain. At some length they were eaters and went into one of the pockets of his Mackinaw, at least toward the end. At first we cut a forked stick to use as a stringer. But when it broke, he put the fish in his pocket.

Tuffy kept telling me about the "flats" where Barger Creek came out of the swamp and widened out. He had once caught an eleven-incher there. But as I said, it was a chilly day. Long before we got to the flats we had both managed to fall in. I fell off a log while trying to cross the creek. Tuffy got wet when a piece of bank gave way and he slipped into the cold water.

After a couple of hours, we were both cold and hungry and decided to call it quits. Tuffy had brought some matches. We had originally planned to roast our catch over a campfire by the creek, but we were too cold. Tuffy cleaned the eight eaters we had kept, stuck them back in his pockets, and we headed back to the farm. To this day I don't know if any were actually seven inches, but a couple were close.

I had eaten brook trout before. We almost always had them when we visited my Uncle Grove. I had never really liked them, though, until that day at the Marlatt farm. It was probably because we were so hungry by the time we got back.

Nobody else was there so Tuffy cooked the trout. He put butter, salt and pepper in an old cast-iron skillet (we called it a spider in those days) and then put in the fish. All eight fit in the one pan. We ate every scrap of meat on those eight fish, even the cheeks. I've loved brook trout ever since.

DIRTIEST BOY(S) IN TOWN

By E. Dan Stevens (2006)

My older sister, Joyce, was not very happy. In fact, she was down-right angry. But Punky and I had brand new silver dollars to spend and so did Austin Briley. I don't know if it was because of Joyce, or not, but the Atlanta Chamber of Commerce didn't have the contest the next year as part of the 4th of July Celebration.

I believe it was 1955. I was twelve that summer and my mother left Joyce in charge while she attended some classes in Ann Arbor. Punky was Rod Marlatt, but I don't think I knew his given name until some years later. He and I did odd jobs around my dad's sawmill during the week and he often stayed at our house when he was in town for some event.

Just as it is now, the 4th of July celebration then was an event. However, then the activities were ongoing over the entire three or four days of the weekend. There was always a large bingo tent on the corner where Forrester's Ford Garage usually displayed their new cars (now next to the State-Wide Real Estate office.) The bingo gave prizes to the winners, not cash, and even we kids could play as long as we had a nickel for a card.

And there was always a baseball game at Doty field on Sunday: Atlanta versus some nearby town. All the town teams played pretty good baseball. Edgar Doty was the owner and manager of the Atlanta team. He always had a few guys from down-state to complement the many good baseball players from Atlanta.

Also, there were games and contests in the park, both in the afternoon and the evening before the fireworks got going.

As part of the 1955 evening events, a contest was announced to determine the dirtiest boy in town. The prize would be a silver dollar. Punky and I decided to enter. We planned to win, agreeing in advance to share the dollar if one was determined to be dirtier than the other by the judges.

Along with nearly every other boy our age in Atlanta, we knew quite a bit already about being dirty. Because of the expected competition, we reckoned that something extra would be needed to win the silver dollar. Well, we found it: used motor oil.

We talked Mr. Utt at the Shell Station into giving us about a gallon of the old oil he had drained from cars when changing oil. Then, dressed in bathing suits, we poured and rubbed the oil all over our bodies. That alone probably would have been sufficient, but we were not done. We found a place along the bank going down to the alley behind the Shell Station where loose black dirt was exposed. We each lay down and rolled in the dark-colored dirt. Of course, the oil was like an adhesive. It didn't take long before we were both dirt over oil. We couldn't lose.

And we didn't. There was only one other boy who was close. Austin Briley was dirt over water. He had jumped in the river and then rolled in dirt while he was still wet. The judges declared all three of us winners and gave us each a silver dollar. Punky and I thought we were dirtier, but since Austin's prize didn't diminish ours, we weren't upset at the decision.

There we were, each with a silver dollar and no clean pocket to put it in. At about that time we realized we might have overdone it a bit. All three of us went in the river to try to get clean (there was no EPA then), but only Austin had any measure of success. For Punky and me, the dirt only came off where we scraped it, and with no soap, the oil hardly came off at all.

We decided that hot water and soap were our only salvation. Had we anticipated my sister's wrath we might have looked for another method, but we ran straight to the old claw-footed bathtub at my house, only a block away.

After an hour or so of scrubbing in hot water with lots of soap we had most of the grime off. (It would be days before all of the oil-smell was gone from my body.) The wash cloths were fatalities and had to be thrown away. Some of the dirt and oil probably went down the drain, but a lot of it stayed on the sides and bottom of the tub. In short, we left the mother of all bathtub rings.

We did recognize the problem and made some effort to clean the tub. Our attempt, however, was not completely successful. The remaining oil ring was still quite pronounced. We decided it would probably come off with time and took off to spend our prize money before the fireworks got started. We went straight to the bingo tent.

By the time we got home from watching the fireworks, Joyce had discovered the remaining bathtub ring and the ruined wash cloths. She was waiting for us. Most people who have known my sister Joyce over the years probably did not know she had a temper. Before that night, neither did I. Suffice it to say that she was very upset and communicated that fact quite well to Punky and me.

As I said before, the 4th of July committee did not have the contest again. I guess that means that Punky, Austin and I still hold the title as the dirtiest boy(s) in town.

THE TENNIS COURT

By E. Dan Stevens (2006)

"I'll take Danny." My heart pounded when I first heard Butch (Ray) Marlatt select me as we all stood around the tennis court while the two older boys chose sides for the game. It was the last pick. A few seconds earlier Kim Bleech had looked my way before selecting Teddy Briley from among the four or five remaining boys wanting to play in the game.

It was 1955 or 1956. For several summers during the mid-50s there was a game nearly every evening on the old tennis court in Atlanta, then located behind the school where the Tri-Township Ambulance garage parking lot is now. We would all congregate there after supper, taking shots whenever we could get our hands on a ball until one of the older boys would announce that it was time for the game.

Incidentally, the game wasn't tennis, it was basketball.

I don't know exactly when the tennis court was built, but it was around during the 40s when my family posed for a picture at a Stevens reunion. Only once did I ever see a tennis net in use on the court, and then for only a few months one summer in the early 60s. Most of the time it was devoted to basketball, but we always called it the tennis court.

The first time I played on it, during fourth grade recess, the baskets were at the sides of the court. The one on the west side was less than the regulation ten feet high, so naturally that was the one we fourth-graders liked best.

Soon after that year, the baskets were moved to the north and south ends by the school and regulation backboards were installed. The old nets, which usually were worn out within weeks after installation, were replaced by ones fabricated from small chain lengths. I am sure that the then new Atlanta High basketball coach, Red (Lyle) McDonnell, was behind the new backboards and goals construction. He wanted his students to play more basketball during the off season. And we did.

Often, our school recess games were played on packed snow during the winter. Learning to shoot and dribble with gloves on took some doing, but we did. As winter subsided, the older boys shoveled the snow so that play was easier. Foster Cameron, who lived across the street from the court, kept an ice spud and coal shovel on his porch to clear ice formed during cold nights after days warm enough to melt the snow banks surrounding the playing area. It was sort of his chore, but we all knew where the tools were in case he wasn't home.

The summertime, though, was when basketball was played on the tennis court many afternoons and almost every evening before it became too dark.

Younger boys would be allowed to shoot around during the warmups, and even play during some late afternoon half-court games, but we were usually on the sidelines watching as the older players went at it in the evening games. I can remember watching Don Savage, Jerry Utt, Sonny and Ron Marlatt, Bob Brooks, and many of the other good Atlanta players from the mid-fifties play nearly every night. Sometimes a couple of Hillman guys would come over to play.

Butch Marlatt, Jim Briley, Kim Bleech, Tuffy Marlatt, Roger Teets, Foster Cameron and others a few years younger played in those games, too. A year or two later they were the juniors and seniors, and we in junior high would be there hoping to get in the game. It often depended on how many showed up.

The older boys would choose sides, but only ten would play in the game. There was no such thing as picking your friend over someone who was a better player. We played to win. The games were usually decided by the first team to make twenty baskets. We were all pretty winded by then.

There were some perils associated with playing basketball on the tennis court. A fall usually meant a pretty serious skin abrasion. In a few places the cement was uneven, particularly near mid-court. Sometimes the ball would go sideways as you dribbled up the court. I remember at least one sprained ankle (me).

But it was a good way to spend a summer evening. Watching was fun when we were younger. Playing in those games as I got older was something I will never forget.

By the time I was a senior, the games still occurred, but were not regular nor were they as well attended. I think it was because by then Atlanta had started a high school football program, and most of us during the summer months were thinking more about blocking and tackling than shooting baskets.

I still can't ride by the ambulance garage without thinking about the old tennis court and those nightly games.

DAVEY'S HAIRCUT

By E. Dan Stevens (2006)

It was the first week of school when Davey explained his problem to us. We were a few of his classmates hanging around in the upstairs hall of the old Atlanta School, the one recently sold on Ebay. The home room bell was still minutes away.

None of us in Atlanta during the late 50's had much money. For Davey's family it was even worse. He and his sister were raised by their single mother, a much more difficult situation then than today.

Davey, however, was no shrinking violet. He was an assertive type, sometimes even boisterous. This attribute often had him in trouble with the principal and his teachers. Often, too, his classmates would find him a little aggravating. But that morning we were all ears, maybe even a little sympathetic.

"I can't even walk past the Sport Shop anymore," he explained. "Mr. Erity will be mad as heck when he sees me."

Glen Erity and his wife Jean owned and operated the Atlanta Sports Shop, a longtime business on Atlanta's main street. It sold all kinds of sporting equipment: guns, fishing gear, basketballs, baseball stuff, etc. It also had nice clothes. I still own a Pendleton wool jacket I purchased there in the early 70's.

Davey continued, "Mr. Erity gave me seventy-five cents so I could get my hair cut before we started school. As you can see, I didn't do it."

We could see. His hair covered his ears. Not too cool in 1957.

"What did you do with the money?" asked David Wilson.

"I spent it on cigarettes and pop." At least Davey was honest. "Can any of you guys lend me seventy-five cents?"

Neither David nor Larry Wilson nor I had an extra seventy-five cents. We each might have been able to contribute a quarter, but we weren't quite that sympathetic.

It was Larry who thought of the solution. "We'll cut your hair, Davey," he offered.

I'm not sure how serious he was at first.

"Do you think you can? Do you think you can make it look good enough for Mr. Erity?" Davey looked at us hopefully.

"Sure we can," Larry answered. "How hard can it be?"

How hard can it be? Pretty hard, I concluded. Glen Boger, the Atlanta barber was good. It would be hard to measure up to his skills.

Larry thought for a few seconds, starting to realize what would be involved. "We would have to give you a brush cut, pretty short," he continued. "Danny has some clippers at his house. We can do it there."

He must have seen the puzzled look on my face. "On the shelf going down to your basement," he said.

"Oh yeah," was all I could say. Larry was referring to the electric sheep shears that my dad occasionally used for his farm animals.

Davey was having second thoughts now. "Are you guys serious? Can you really do it? I don't want to look like a bum."

David Wilson, probably not then knowing that Larry was referring to sheep shears, clinched the deal. "Davey, you look like a bum now. I promise that we'll make you look better. You'll be able to go by the Sports Shop again. Mr. Erity will never know the difference."

So it was that we set about to solve Davey Moore's haircut dilemma. We made arrangements to do it that afternoon after school.

Behind my house was an old cement building which had once housed the water pumps that Grove Rouse had used for the Hardware Store next door. We kids used it as a clubhouse of sorts. David, Larry and I met Davey there right after school. I got the sheep shears and ran an extension cord from my back porch.

We had Davey sit on one of the old pump blocks and brought out the shears. His eyes got big, but he said nothing. He was committed.

We decided that Larry had the steadiest hand so he turned on the shears and prepared to cut. The shears were loud. Now Davey was clearly worried, but he stayed. Larry was doing a good job. He trimmed the sides as short as the shears would cut and then eyed the top of Davey's head.

This is where things started to go south. In those days a true brush cut meant a flat cut of hair about three-quarters inch long. The hair was held straight up by the application of a wax product. Davey's hair was laying over so we decided to apply the wax first. His hair was still too long so David and I held it up with combs while Larry cut.

Everything seemed to be going well. Larry was making a nice flat cut and it was about the right length. Davey, however, was getting impatient. As Larry was about halfway across the top, Davey looked up. The sheep shears kept cutting, all the way to his scalp.

There was no way to hide the deep "V" in Davey's hair. The skin head look was not then in vogue so we were forced to leave well enough alone.

Except for the "V", the haircut looked pretty good. I don't know if Mr. Erity ever noticed the "V", but we did at school for the next few weeks.

Davey's family moved away after that school year and I didn't see him again for many years. In the late 70's I ran into him at Walker's Inn. He was passing through. We exchanged histories and stories for an hour or so. He was living in Alaska and doing well. Neither of us mentioned the haircut.

NASTY BRILEY

By E. Dan Stevens (2006)

"Hello, I'm Austin Junior Nasty Briley. What's your name?"

He was eight and I was nine. He lived two houses away from the Charles and Stella Brown farmhouse which we rented that first summer my dad moved us back to Atlanta. He quickly explained that I wasn't expected to call him by the whole name. He would answer to Austin or Junior or Nasty.

Thus began my friendship with Austin Briley, Jr., which was ended only by his death a few weeks ago. We didn't grow up being best friends or anything like that, but we grew up together in Atlanta and he was a part of a lot of things that happened in my life over the years.

That first summer we spent many afternoons playing and gigging frogs in the pond behind the Brown house. I am sure my mother probably got tired of frying them, but we never got tired of eating frog legs from our catches.

I remember the 1952 Christmas Eve. His mother, Almeda, told us that at midnight the barnyard animals would all kneel in celebration. There was a cattle barn across the road from his house so Austin and I made plans to meet there at 11:45. It didn't happen because we both fell asleep too early. We talked about doing it again for several years, but to this day I have been unable to verify Mrs. Briley's story.

Austin was a lot like his Uncle Eldon (Dobbyn), at times almost larger than life. He always seemed to rise to the occasion. I vividly remember his shot from the corner as overtime expired that won our first basketball game my senior year (his junior year) against Gaylord St. Mary.

In football, he played defensive end. He would often say, "Nobody runs the ball around this side." I think that's when I learned that it's not bragging if it's fact.

Another time during our high school years Austin decided to fish Hay Meadow Creek upstream from Reiman Road, a nearly impossible task because of the thick tag alders most of the way. I dropped him off and later picked him up at Kellyville Road. He had ten of the nicest brook trout I had ever seen, but he was so tired he could hardly walk or talk, the latter a real anomaly.

Many of the things that happened in my life as I grew up involved Austin in one way or another. He was a part of two of the five stories I've written so far in this series and was a part of many more not yet written.

After school we went separate ways. He became a Marine. Some years later we both returned and worked in Montmorency County. Our children went to school together during those years. Later, we both moved to Florida. I am sorry to say that during the fifteen years we lived less than sixty miles apart we only got together once or twice. I kept up with him more during later years through his sister, Tess. It was she who told me about his illness two years ago.

Not long after that conversation I was driving past Venice, Florida, where he lived. On impulse I turned off at a Venice exit and looked up his number in the book. He answered my call and gave me directions to his home.

A flagpole was prominent in his yard; the American flag was on top, the Marine Corps flag flying beneath. He was waiting in the doorway with a big smile. It was like we had been together the day before. He was the same.

He had to use a walker because his heel had been surgically removed only a few days before. Nevertheless, he practically ran with the thing. We sat by his pool and talked about our lives and our children and our mutual friends and about Atlanta. At noon he offered me a drink. I accepted. He had one too.

All too soon I had to leave to keep an obligation in Tallahassee. It was the last time I saw or talked to Austin. It wasn't the last time I thought about him, though. Austin Junior Nasty Briley is inseparable from the memories and experiences of growing up in Atlanta, Michigan, during the fifties.

RIVER ICE

By E. Dan Stevens (2006)

From my experience with grandchildren, mine and others, it seems that nowadays once Thanksgiving is over all kids' thoughts turn to Christmas. T'wasn't the case during the fifties in Atlanta, Michigan. Then, after Thanksgiving and deer season were behind us, our focus shifted to ice.

Although the exact date varied from year to year, sometime during the first half of December the Thunder Bay River Dam Pond began to freeze over. The bays and other areas away from the old river channel were first, but it didn't take long for the entire pond to become ice-covered once winter took over. We kids were testing it as soon as the first one or two inches of ice appeared. When it reached four inches thick, we were ready to skate.

The new ice was the best; when we were lucky, we might go a week or ten days before any snow accumulated to limit our range up and down the pond. When snow did come, the older boys would shovel a rink area in front of the park, a hundred feet square or so. I vividly remember Donny Dice skating and pushing a big curved snow shovel across the ice so fast that the snow flew away from the shovel as if from a snow plow on a county truck.

Usually we hauled a couple of old logs out to the rink to serve as benches to change into our skates. We always hauled wood for a fire, often on an old toboggan someone left at the rink. I was at first amazed that the fire didn't melt through the ice, but it didn't.

The skating usually lasted well into January. It was ended by either too much snow to keep shoveling or by a thaw that would result in rough ice. Also, more snow meant other things to do like sledding at the Davis hill and skiing at Sheridan Valley. While it lasted though, we would skate most afternoons after school and lots of the evenings, plus all day Saturday and Sunday afternoon.

The week after Christmas was a prime time for skating on the Thunder Bay Pond. Many received new skates for Christmas, new for us at least. We were growing boys and girls, after all, so there was a brisk business in used skates. The girls and a few boys had figure skates. Most of the boys had hockey skates.

There was skating every night during that week with big bonfires; all of us were enjoying our new skates and just being on the ice with most every kid between eight and sixteen from town and the surrounding areas.

Snowmobiles were still years in the future then. The only sounds we would hear during those cold nights on the ice were the sounds of our skates, our talking and laughter, and the occasional groan from the expansion and shifting of the ice.

But skating wasn't the only activity on the Thunder Bay River ice. There were always at least a half-dozen fish shanties on the pond along the old river channel. Most of us had at least occasional access to one or more of them. Some were owned by a friend's father or older brother, and we could often use them when the father or brother wasn't.

We speared northern pike (or at least tried, as was the case with me) and caught perch and bluegills with a hook and line. It was fun watching for fish through the ice hole. Each shanty had either a kerosene stove or a wood stove and was a warm place to be on a cold winter day. Some of the older boys would take their girlfriends fishing with them in their shanties. I've heard rumors that the shanty could be a pretty romantic place!

We also witnessed the end of an era during those years: ice harvesting. The ice you buy today at the local store or gas station is made at an ice factory with large refrigeration equipment and distributed in bags of cubes or blocks to ice bins at the stores. Not so in those days.

Even though the icebox was pretty much a thing of the past in most homes, ice blocks were still available. I can remember the Gulf Station (now Betty and Bucky's), Reiman's Corner and Wilson's Grocery as places that sold ice. Each had a small icehouse outside. The ice was covered with sawdust which kept it from thawing. The storekeeper would use an ice pick to halve or quarter the block to the size you wanted and ice tongs to lift it into your chest or box.

The blocks of ice came from the Thunder Bay River Dam Pond winter ice cover. Jim Kent, Bruce Kent, Sr., and their sons did the harvesting. We kids were spectators and sometimes helped. They would start cutting and loading ice when it got to be twelve or fourteen inches thick.

A large circular sawmill-type saw powered by an old car motor mounted on a steel sled was used to cut the ice. Jim or Jack or Bruce or Don Renodin would use it to cut along parallel lines about sixteen inches apart over a large area of the ice from which the snow had been removed. Perpendicular lines were then cut to make blocks.

The floating blocks of ice would be pushed with pike poles to a chain link conveyer which lifted them to the back of a truck. Often Jim would ask me and other kids to help direct the blocks through the water with poles to the conveyer. His son, Jack, and Bruce Jr. were on the truck with tongs stacking the blocks for the trip to Jim's icehouse.

Larry Wilson recently told me about helping his dad get ice from the icehouse for resale at their store. They would have to dig through the insulating sawdust to get to the ice. The icehouse was located in Jim Kent's yard, just east of the intersection of Baker Road and M-32.

It wasn't all we did in winter, but river ice was a big part of growing up in Atlanta, Michigan.

MEMORIES OF CHRISTMAS

By E. Dan Stevens (2006)

I looked at the clock as I answered the old crank phone on our kitchen wall. It was 10:30, Christmas morning, 1955. I wondered which operator was working on the holiday, Mrs. Huntley or Mrs. Gunther. Or it might have been Mrs. Blamer, the owner.

"Hello."

"Hi, what did you get?" It was Darrell Briley.

"I got the BB gun I wanted, and Bobby gave me a watch." Bob, my brother, was a freshman in college, home for the holidays. "How about you?"

"New skates and an F-86 model. The model is from Dennis," Darrell answered. Dennis is his older brother; the F-86 was the Air Force's best jet-fighter. "Have you had breakfast?"

"Yeah."

"My mother's making hot chocolate. Come on over. Bring your gun for me to see."

"Okay," I said. Marion Briley made the best hot chocolate in town. I grabbed my coat and ran the block and a half to their house.

It was one of those memories that has been with me over the years, walking into the Briley house through the kitchen on that holiday morning, the smells of cookies and Christmas dinner in the oven, the physical warmth of the house after running through the morning chill, the warmth of my friend and his family, and the two cups of hot chocolate sitting on the kitchen dinette that Mrs. Briley had made for Darrell and me.

Their house always seemed to be warmer than most on cold, windy days. It might have been because of its coal furnace, one of the last in Atlanta.

Another Christmas Day memory is from the year I received a camera as my present. I went over to show Bob Teets, and he and I took lots of pictures of the ice and snow along Hay Meadow Creek behind his house. (It's hard to forget that day because I keep running across those pictures every now and then.)

Plenty of other memories are with me from those Christmas seasons past in Atlanta, Michigan. Like Christmas carols on old 78's that could be heard all along the main street from speakers atop Forrester's Ford Garage; and the large Christmas tree in the used car lot across the street; and the gathering there of students and parents after the school Christmas concert to light the tree and sing a few more holiday songs; (My cousin Sylvia told me the other day that she remembers how dressed up everyone was for those school concerts and the festivities around the tree.) and caroling with the Pilgrim Fellowship youth group from our church under the leadership of June Chadwick and Sis McMurphy; (I have this distinct memory of singing at the Downing house and Mrs. Downing bringing out some cookies for us afterwards.) and other groups caroling at our house; and white-bearded Billy Dean, the perfect Santa Claus; and the pageant we put on for our parents at church.

I also remember going with my mother and my sister Joyce to Alpena for the clothes portion of our Christmas shopping. In those days our parents only gave us one present for our fun, like a BB gun or a camera. But we would get two or three other "presents", always articles of clothing or boots that we needed anyway. It must have been in Alpena that I saw my first Salvation Army bell-ringer because now when I see one I invariably have a flashback to the one standing outside the old J.C. Penny store in the old Alpena downtown.

Of course, we also did some Christmas shopping at Joe Tunnicliff's Drug Store, Erity's Sport Shop, Briley's Hardware and Peterson's General Store in Atlanta. Also, Hillman had Vanderveer's and O'Farrells and other nice stores. But as I said, we didn't get piles of presents like kids do these days.

And cutting the tree. You could buy a tree at my Uncle Olin's house, but most of our parents had access to a balsam or spruce on their land or a friend's, and it was great fun for us to help pick out and cut our family's Christmas tree for the year.

And Christmas day. It was wonderful having older siblings back from college or working downstate. Dad always fixed us a big pancake breakfast after we opened our presents.

Then visiting back and forth with our friends to share, or at least showoff, our newly acquired treasures. And the big Christmas dinner which Mother prepared.

However, that wasn't all. Our week after Christmas was filled with activity, too. Ice skating, sometimes sledding and skiing, and at least once, a hay ride on an old set of sleighs organized by several parents kept us busy one very enjoyable evening.

One year Dad took Darrell and me to camp out at one of his old cabins for a couple of days after Christmas. The cabin was heated by an old wood stove, and we cooked on a propane burner. We took our sleds but the snow was too deep and fluffy to go downhill. Finally Dad cut two long poles and pulled us behind his pickup on the packed snow of the trail going to and from the cabin, using the poles to prevent us from sliding close to the vehicle in case he had to stop quickly. It was fun, but we were soon caked with ice and snow from head to toe. Thawing out afterwards next to the cabin's wood stove might have been more enjoyable than the sledding itself.

Christmas season then didn't last as long, and for those of us in Montmorency County wasn't nearly as commercial, but it was a great time for us kids, and I think for our parents as well. We all felt blessed. I think we were.

TROUT FISHING WITH TUFFY - PART 2

By E. Dan Stevens (2007)

Visionaries, pioneers, ahead of our time? I don't believe Tuffy was exactly thinking in those terms when he said, "Let's see if we can get to McCormick Lake. Turn here."

"Okay," I answered as I slowed to look at the snow-covered road. It had been plowed earlier that winter, but was now covered with the same 8-10 inches of new snow which we had already been driving through for much of the day. Duck soup for my 1937 Chevrolet. It was the best snow car I've ever owned.

We had spent most of that Saturday ice fishing at a few hard to get to lakes with only limited success. We had maybe a half-dozen pan fish to show for our efforts. But we were having fun breaking trail through the new snow with the old Chevrolet.

In those days, ice fishing was not allowed on McCormick Lake nor any other lake which was a designated trout lake. I don't know if Tuffy originally had fishing in mind when he suggested we turn toward the lake or whether he just wanted to see if we could get there through the snow. In any case, fate intervened.

For reasons that I will explain in a later Tale, the normal conflicts between parental values and peer pressures that most teenagers experience were magnified many times over for me when it came to hunting and fishing laws.

The '37 Chevy knifed through the snow easily as we drove toward the public landing site on the west shore of McCormick Lake. I stopped the car as the lake came into view. From there we would have to descend down a slight incline to the flat area that was the parking lot for the access site.

"What do you think?" I asked.

"We can't turn around here," Tuffy observed. "We either have to back out or go down to the parking lot to turn around. I think you can get a running start on the flat part and make it back up the hill without too much trouble."

"Okay," I said as I eased out the clutch and the car started down the hill.

That's when fate intervened. We made it down to the parking lot okay, but as I started to turn around I backed right into a ditch which had been hidden by the drifted snow. Try as we might the car couldn't get enough traction to pull out of the ditch. After about twenty minutes, we admitted defeat.

It would have been a four-mile walk through deep snow back to the highway so I offered to cross the lake and climb the hill to the Paulson home, one of only two on the lake at that time.

We were pretty sure they had a phone. Tuffy, not one to just stand around, announced that he would see if trout really would bite under the ice while I was gone. He grabbed a spud and a pole and walked with me about half-way across the lake before he stopped to spud a hole in the ice.

I continued on. It was quite a grind to climb the hill on the east side of the lake through the snow to the Paulson house. It was even worse to discover that no one was home. As I was contemplating my next step, I noticed a light through the trees to the south. Although I didn't know them as well as I did the Paulsons, I hurried toward the light at the Krentel's <u>house</u>. They were home and graciously invited me to use their phone.

I called Jim Basch. Luckily, he and Austin Briley had been working on Jim's doodlebug, an old truck that had been cut down to tractor-like proportions. They had just gotten it running and agreed to come help us get unstuck. They were at Big Rock so it was about a ten-mile trip for them in an open and topless cab on a cold winter day.

I thanked Mr. and Mrs. Krentel and again answered their questions about why we happened to be stuck at the public access site. I didn't mention that Tuffy was fishing.

I worked my way back down the hill and across the lake to where Tuffy was standing by a hole in the ice. He had three nice rainbow trout lying in the snow. He had proven they would bite. Now we just had to determine if they were good eating in the winter.

By the time we had wound his line on the short ice fishing pole and walked back across to the west shore, we could hear Jim's doodlebug heading our way. In short order with the doodlebug pulling on a chain and Austin and Tuffy pushing, the old Chevy came out of the ditch.

By then it was almost dark. The doodlebug, with no lights, followed us out to M-32 and stuck closely behind us on the highway to Big Rock. Austin, who could have ridden with Tuffy and me in the relative warmth of the car, chose to stay with Jim on the open doodlebug. At the Big Rock store we all had a pop and tried to explain to Mr. Basch why we happened to be at the McCormick Lake access site. We didn't mention the trout.

Although the world probably didn't know it at the time, Tuffy and I were in the vanguard that day. Only a year or two later the Conservation Department opened the trout lakes to ice fishing.

But that wasn't the end of the saga for me. In a later tale I will relate the rest of the story.

FISHING WITH TUFFY - BACKLASH

By E. Dan Stevens (2007)

It was a bad day for me at the barbershop. There was only one barber in Atlanta during those days. He was in the same small building on the main street as is one of the barbershops today. It was next to Gavine's Cafe and was the last building on the block until Merv and Helen Davis built an appliance store on the other side (now Huston Real Estate.) Lots of information, maybe even a few rumors, changed hands at the barbershop. I think that the final battle of the great river war was concocted between Benny Thompson and Terry Brooks one day as they were both waiting for a haircut.

The first barber I remember was Nick Kilburg, already up in years by the time I came along. He was soft-spoken, a true gentleman, and especially nice to us kids. Sometime in the late fifties he sold the shop to Glen Boger and retired.

Glen came from Grayling and was an avid trout fisherman. When he wasn't busy cutting hair, he was tying trout-flies on a vice and other fly-tying equipment he kept on the counter behind one of the two barber chairs. Glen was willing to teach anyone willing to learn the art of tying flies. I was willing, but my hands were too klutzy. Even though I tried, I was never able to tie a fly that would catch trout.

Which gets me to my bad day - well almost. I should also explain why I was so considerably conflicted between my parental values and peer values when it came to fish and game laws while I was growing up in Montmorency County. You see, my father who was born and raised in the Kellyville community, the son of a man who for several years made his living as a hunter of wild game year-round to feed the lumber camps, was one of the first recipients of a Masters Degree in wildlife management from the University of Michigan. Later, he was a leader in bringing scientific game management programs and laws to North Carolina while he was a professor at North Carolina State University. He was also a missionary for strict enforcement of game and fish laws. It would have been a toss-up in my house as to whether I would have been punished more for robbing a gas station or for violating a game or fish law.

On the other hand, many of the old-timers in Atlanta had lived much of their lives without any game or fish laws and even then during the fifties augmented their provisions with wild game as needed, without regard to seasons. Certainly the community norm would have considered food necessity and other factors to be more important than the strict enforcement of game and fish laws. In fact, many of my friends and their families considered game and fish laws to be something akin to guidelines to be followed only when convenient.

You can see the dilemma I sometimes faced, like when Tuffy decided to see if rainbow trout would bite through the ice while we were stuck in the snow at McCormick Lake. Not such an unreasonable use of our time while we waited for help in my mind, but likely to have been severely condemned by my dad.

Now for my bad day. It started okay when I walked into the barbershop a week or so after Tuffy and I had gotten the '37 Chevy stuck at McCormick Lake. There was one person in the barber chair when I came in so I sat in one of the chairs along the wall to wait my turn. While I was still waiting, Jack Huntly came in and sat beside me. Jack was the local game warden, known by most to be strict but fair.

After a few pleasantries among Jack, Glen Boger, the other customer and me, Jack looked over at me and said, "Danny, I heard that you and Tuffy and Tom Barry were fishing trout the other day out on McCormick Lake."

I was stunned and probably looked it. On the other hand, Tom Barry had not been with us that day. I had heard that some of the other guys had been ice fishing on Clear Lake, another trout lake, and thought that Tom might have been one of them, but he definitely hadn't been with us on McCormick Lake.

I recovered enough to answer, "That's not true, Mr. Huntly."

I thought I wasn't lying because the part about Tom being there wasn't correct.

The conversation continued in the same vein for a while with Glen Boger joining in. Because of their belief that Tom Barry was with us, I could somewhat truthfully deny the accusation. When they didn't mention Tom, I tried not to answer.

Finally it was my turn to get in the chair. Just as Glen finished adjusting the barber cloth around my neck, my father walked into the shop and sat down next to Jack Huntly to wait his turn. I was nervous and trapped if the conversation about McCormick Lake continued.

To my great relief, Dad and Jack started talking about something else entirely. However, Glen Boger wasn't through with the story. I like to think it was because he was new in town and didn't understand my father's passion about game and fish laws.

Just as I began to think I was out of the woods, Glen said loudly and with amusement in his voice, "Ross, did Danny give you some of the trout he caught through the ice at McCormick Lake? He wouldn't give Jack or me any."

My heart sank.

Dad asked, "What trout?"

"Ask Jack," Glen answered.

Dad turned toward Jack. "Was Danny ice fishing at McCormick Lake?" His voice was tense.

Jack, who did know Dad and his devotion to game laws, didn't hesitate as he answered, "No Ross, I was just teasing him. I don't have any reason to believe he was fishing out there."

Glen Boger looked perplexed. I was relieved and got out of there as soon as my haircut was finished, very grateful to Jack Huntly for not relaying his suspicions to my father. I wouldn't have been able to tell Dad a half-truth had he ever questioned me.

As years went by I came to consider Jack Huntly as a good friend. That afternoon was the beginning.

THE GREAT PORCUPINE HUNT

By E. Dan Stevens (2007)

Game poles have long been a tradition in Montmorency County. Many of us remember old pictures from hunting camps featuring hunters proudly standing with their guns cradled in arm, their bagged deer hanging from a horizontal pole behind.

The first buck pole that I remember in Atlanta was in front of Joe Tunnicliff's Drug Store. I could see it from my living room window. Every night during the first week of deer season the hunters would congregate around the pole admiring and discussing the deer and occasional bear and coyote hanging from the pole. The Chamber of Commerce gave prizes for the first and largest bucks and the largest bear.

The buck pole was later moved to the parking lot next to Claude Mowery's real estate office where it remains today. The elk version is of much more recent origin.

Which brings us to the county's only (I'm quite sure) porcupine pole. Jimmy Durkee, Larry Wilson, David Wilson and I were quite proud of it; my dad's feelings about it were very different.

The great porcupine hunt was not a planned event. It occurred because we couldn't find any rabbits or other game that weekend. It was late February, either 1956 or 1957. We got a lot of snow that year, but had several days of thaw in mid-February. When the seasonal cold returned the snow formed a thick crust that easily supported a person's weight.

During that week in school, the four of us decided to go on a weekend hunting trip at my dad's cabin. The cabin was located on Camp 8 Road about a mile north of Camp 8 Corners. It was next door to his sawmill and had been built with materials from the mill. Dad and the rest of the sawmill crew had their lunch in the cabin, often eating a stew they would place on the wood stove in the morning to be hot by lunchtime.

The cabin had four rooms. The only appliances were the wood stove for heating, a pitcher pump and sink, and a bottled gas range; no electricity. We also had an old crank phonograph that played 78 rpm records which had belonged to my grandmother.

We bought and scrounged our food Friday after school and got one of our parents to give us a ride to the cabin. We took sleeping bags, some spare clothes and our guns. Most of us had .22's but Jimmy also brought a .410 shotgun.

Dad had left a fire in the wood stove and the pump primed so it was easy to move in and make supper that first night; I'm pretty sure it was something one of our mothers made ahead of time that we just warmed up.

The next morning wasn't as easy. First, one of us had to leave his warm sleeping bag and start a new fire in the wood stove. Then we made breakfast from scratch, scrambled eggs and bacon, and maybe pancakes. Then the worst thing, dishes. In truth, we probably stacked them in the sink with a vow to do them after lunch.

Saturday morning - we decided to hunt the cedar swamp behind the cabin. When we returned about 11:00, we had not seen one rabbit, nor had we seen any tracks on the crusted snow.

We had bologna sandwiches for lunch. Easy and not too many new dirty dishes added to the pile. Afterward we stoked the fire and headed away from the swamp and up into the hardwood covered hills across the road from the cabin.

The thick crust made it easy to traverse the deep snow. Again, no sign of rabbits.

It was Larry who first spotted the animal droppings under a hemlock, the only species of evergreen tree to be seen in the hardwood forest. "Look, something's up that tree."

"Probably a porcupine," Jimmy said as he walked over to take a closer look. He was the most woods-savvy among us.

"I'm sure it is," I added. "My dad says they are killing the few hemlocks we have left. It's okay with him if we shoot porcupines that are up in hemlock trees."

"Are they good to eat?" asked David.

"I've heard they can be eaten in an emergency." Jimmy was circling the hemlock trying to see up through the thick foliage. "Hey, there are two of them in this tree, no, three I think."

"Since we aren't getting any rabbits, let's make this a porcupine hunt," Larry offered by way of a decision.

Soon there were three dead porcupines lying on the snow under that first hemlock tree. Every hemlock we inspected after that had at least one porcupine, often two. Only that first had three, but it wasn't long before we had brought down thirteen porcupines.

I don't remember when we decided to make a porcupine pole along the road in front of the cabin, but we did. It might have been because we were determined to see if they were edible which would mean taking at least one back to the cabin.

In any event, we went back and found a roll of binder twine at the sawmill and fashioned a couple of sticks into yokes. Two of us could drag three porcupines tied to the yokes by the binder twine. It took two trips by all of us to get the carcasses back to the cabin. We then hoisted them by the twine over the small timber we had affixed between two trees along the road, our own version of the game pole.

Jim did skin one of the porkys, very carefully, and we boiled it for a couple of hours that evening. I think three of us had a small taste. Larry watched us and declined his share. Maybe it wasn't seasoned just right, but it tasted a lot like wood. We were happy to throw it out and feast on the hot dogs that were cooking on another burner.

Someone else must have picked us up Sunday because my dad didn't see our game pole until Monday when he went to work at the mill. He was still fuming when he got home that night. "Did you ever think about what's going to happen when those porcupines thaw in front of my sawmill this spring?" he asked.

We hadn't thought of that. I was so distracted by his question that I forgot to tell him about all the hemlock trees we saved.

MY 1937 CHEVROLET

By E. Dan Stevens (2007)

      The following verses were written for an assignment in Mr. (Lyle) McDonnell's American literature class during my senior year at Atlanta High:

"In the year of '37
From the factories of Detroit
Came a thing itself from heaven,
A new Chevy for exploit.

'Twas a fine car in the making,
Skill used here and there,
Like a cake made for baking
T'was a car made for wear.

Two decades, three years later
Now old, has had its wear
Has some teenagers for to cater
Some who drive with love and care.

I'm the owner of this car
It's the beauty of my day,
Though it won't go too far
People like it, so they say."

It really wasn't intended to be my car. Dad bought it from Mr. Weaver (Vienna Township) for twenty-five dollars. He planned to use it as his woods car, but he never got the chance. He made the mistake of letting me drive it the day he brought it home and never really got it back. I don't remember our conversation exactly, but from then on it was pretty much my car.

At times, not just mine either. It was somewhat of a community car since it ended up as the transportation for many of us teenagers during those years. We would often pile in and drive to Hillman to see a movie. I remember once collecting pop bottles to buy gas. We took the bottles to Al Hamilton and George Pinchock's Shell Station and redeemed them directly for fuel into the gas tank. It was enough to get to Hillman and back. Fortunately, Mr. and Mrs. Benac only charged twenty cents for student admission to the theater.

Our youth group at the church, Pilgrim Fellowship, often raised money by putting on a supper in the church basement. The '37 Chevy was our mode of advertising. We painted the pertinent information about the supper on the black car with white shoe polish and drove around town all afternoon honking the horn to bring attention to our project. It always seemed to work well, except for one Saturday when it rained cats and dogs. I guess you know that shoe polish is water-soluble.

It was also a great snow car. Several of us liked to go snowshoeing in the pristine winter wilderness around Atlanta and often did on Sunday afternoons. There were no snowmobiles in those days, and we could go a long way without seeing any sign of other humans in the deep snow. The '37 Chevy was most often our transportation over the back roads to where we would begin our snowshoe trek.

One time we decided to have a winter picnic at my dad's cabin on Camp 8 road. When we got to Camp 8 Corner, we discovered that the road north to the cabin had not been plowed recently and was covered with ten inches, or so, of new snow. We left the other car there and nine of us (plus the picnic supplies) crammed into the '37 for the final mile to the cabin. It got there quite easily. Turning around was somewhat hectic, but we had plenty of people to push.

The '37 Chevrolet was a rugged car and got plenty of use during the almost two years of hauling me and my friends around the county. It was the mainstay of our transportation for the Can't Hardly Lumber Company crew. Tuffy and I were in it when we got stuck at McCormick Lake. It took us trout fishing all over the county. And lots more.

We weren't always too gentle with it either. One spring day Jim Basch, Bill Valentine and I made great sport out of racing through the few snowdrifts that remained in the hollows of fields otherwise bare after the thaw. The snow really flew as the car hit a drift at about 30 mph. In almost every case the momentum of the car would carry us through the wet snow. I say 'almost' because in a field just east of Big Rock we met our match. The drift was much deeper than it looked and the others we had crashed through. Halfway across the '37 just sank.

There was no way we could dig or push it out. Jim's doodlebug must have been on the blink because we had to go all the way to Kellyville to get Bill's father's tractor to pull us out.

Fortunately, we had lots of help to repair and maintain the old car in spite of our sometimes abusive use. Al and George let us use the Shell Station garage and tools whenever they weren't otherwise occupied with paying customers.

Once when I drove the '37 to pick up some parts for my dad at Alvin Bartow's tractor and implement firm in Hillman, the mechanic there told me its engine sounded like it had some burned valves. He offered to grind the valves for next to nothing. It was almost closing time, but with Alvin's permission he stayed after and did the work then and there. It did run a lot better on the way home.

In those days not many of us possessed an automobile during our teen years and nobody had a new one. I think Jimmy Utt's '56 Ford might have been the newest, and it was a junker that he rebuilt himself. Larry Wilson had a Model A Ford for a while. I can't remember many others. We mostly relied on borrowing a parent's car. David Wilson used his grandmother's 1955 Chevrolet pretty much all the time.

But we shared a lot. When Karen Davis, Mary Ann Blamer, Jenny Benson, Mary Lou Paul, Claudia Cameron and my cousin Sylvia got together and wanted to go somewhere, the '37 Chevy and I were pretty much on call.

Incidentally, Mr. McDonnell gave me an 'A' for my poem.

STEVE'S PLACE

By E. Dan Stevens (2007)

The phone conversations probably went something like this: "Hello, Danny, this is Mary Lou. Do you understand the trig problem Mr. Currie gave us today?"

"Not really, do you?" I answered.

"That's why I'm calling. Do you think Darrell does?"

"I'll call him and see. Do you want to meet at Steve's to work on it?"

"Sounds okay. I'll be there in twenty minutes. See you then."

That call was from Mary Lou Paul. I hung up and phoned the Briley house. "Hello, Darrell. Mary Lou and I are going to meet at Steve's in twenty minutes to work on the trig problem. Do you want to come?"

"Funny, I've just been talking with Danny Walker about the assignment and we had just decided to get together," he answered. "We'll both meet you there."

It's J D's Pizza Place these days and has been for the last twenty plus years, but in the later 50's and early 60's it was Steve's Place. Steve was Steve Fournier, the grandfather of several of my friends and a long-time businessman in Atlanta. He was also a sweetheart of a man who cared not only about the well-being of his grandchildren, but about the rest of us who were growing up in the Atlanta area during those years. There is no doubt in my mind, nor by anyone I've talked with about it over the years, that he built Steve's Place just for us.

I was lucky to be a contemporary of several of his grandchildren. Larry and Mary Ann Blamer (now Marlatt), Julia Blamer (now Walker), and his namesake, Steve Englehart were the closest of them to my age. Larry and Mary Ann Blamer were brother and sister, but were cousins to Julie. Their fathers, Bob and Homer Blamer, were brothers who married two of the Fournier sisters, Gene and Connie. The other Fournier sister, Maxine, broke with tradition to marry Bill Englehart.

Steve Fournier was a character from my father's bedtime stories before I ever met him. Dad had worked for him after school during the early 20's when he owned Hotel Steve, the predecessor of what was known as the Atlanta Hotel when I was growing up. Dad rode his horse, Bucko, from his home on Kellyville Road to attend the high school in Atlanta. He arranged to leave the horse during the school day at the hotel stable and worked there after school to pay the boarding fee. Tales of his experiences with Bucko and while working for Mr. Fournier were standards of his bedtime repertoire.

I don't know when I connected the dots between those early stories and the man I knew through my friends as "Dad Steve", but I can remember playing among the large white pines in his yard with Mary Ann and Julia and being invited in by "Grandma Ethelyn" for milk and cookies.

Their house was on the corner where the Post Office is now and their yard extended to where the current Tribune Building is located.

Steve built the building for the Place with his own hands. Oh, he had lots of aid when needed from sons-in-law and grandchildren and others around town. He was sort of like Tom Sawyer in that we all deemed it a privilege to be allowed to help with his construction projects. I can remember nailing rolled roofing on an earlier building he built, now First Choice Real Estate, as well as on the building that became Steve's Place.

Steve's Place was a project he initiated to give Atlanta teenagers someplace to go in the evenings and something to do. It had a snack bar along the front and left side as you walked in and some tables and chairs in front. The back part of the large room had a jukebox and an area for dancing. Two or three pinball machines were along the back wall. The only other rooms were two bathrooms at the end of the snack bar.

He served hot dogs and hamburgers, pop and ice cream, and some other snacks. I think he had a mixer for malts and shakes as well. The prices were just enough to cover costs, I'm sure.

As many of us in high school regularly or occasionally went downtown for lunch, Steve provided an alternative just across the street from the school. The Place was often crowded during lunch hour as Steve and Ethelyn served up their fare to the hungry students. On especially busy days their granddaughters, Mary Ann and Julie, and sometimes their friends, would chip in to take orders and deliver hamburgers to the tables.

Steve himself operated the Place most evenings until eleven, or so, and later on weekends. It was pretty much open every evening, but on occasion we would go there only to find it closed. We would know that Steve had a cold or the flu or was otherwise unable to be there. Disappointed as we were those nights, we were aware that the Place would be open again when Steve was up and about.

We went there for many reasons, and yes, studying was one of them. Mr. (Archie) Currie, our math and physics teacher often gave us assignments which required a group effort to solve and Steve's Place was a perfect place to meet for that purpose.

We could also listen to the jukebox, dance or just chat with our friends. Steve was himself a person we teenagers liked to be around and his attitude spilled over to his patrons. I don't remember anything approaching a fight or other confrontational situation ever occurring at Steve's. We probably knew that he would "bar" any participants and none of us wanted that.

So, solving Mr. Currie's math assignment maybe wasn't the only reason we met at Steve's Place, but it was a great story to tell our parents as we headed there.

THE FREE SHOW

By E. Dan Stevens (2007)

It was free for everyone on Wednesday nights during the summer. Most of us walked the half-mile, or so, west along M-32 from Atlanta. Some of the older kids and a few adults would come in cars, but because they had to park behind the projector van, I don't think they could hear very well. Maybe it didn't matter that much to them.

It was the free show, outside in a field and pretty much an institution for us in Atlanta and some other small towns without movie theaters during the fifties. As I said earlier, our night was Wednesday. The show started at dark. It was probably a good thing we didn't have daylight savings time in those days.

Unlike Lewiston with its roller rink and Hillman with its regular movie theater, Atlanta never really had an established entertainment attraction for children and young adults. Not that we didn't have some people making efforts in that direction. The V.F.W. Post showed movies at its hall four or five nights a week for several years during the late forties and early fifties in a theater-like setting, complete with a popcorn and refreshment stand.

I was told by John Weber the other day at Red's Barber Shop that during the thirties Claude Sherwood showed movies some evenings in the study hall of the old high school and that in later years a gentleman from Lincoln, Fred Blumer, brought a movie to the Atlanta School Community Building every Thursday night.

Later that same day I ran into Helen Waite at the grocery parking lot. She remembered that Mr. Blumer continued bringing movies to Atlanta even after the Community Building was destroyed by fire in 1943. His new venue was the back room of the Atlanta Hotel. She also confirmed my vague memory that her two brothers, Woodrow and Leslie Wilson, started construction on a movie theater during the 40's on land now occupied by the Atlanta Motel. For one reason or another, that project was never completed.

But we did have the free show. It took place in the field across M-32 from the Full Gospel Church, just east of the social services building. The proprietor, who went from town to town in his 40's panel van, had erected a permanent wooden frame on which he stretched the movie screen for the night's feature. He parked his van about forty feet away with the back facing the screen. He had only to open the van's rear door to allow the 16mm projector mounted in the van to do its work.

If I ever knew his name, I've forgotten it, but I do remember that he was fairly on in years during the early fifties when I was a regular at the free show. There was often a woman with him, I assume his wife, who helped with the popcorn machine and the inventory of candy bars and pop he sold. Oh yes, not everything was free. The pop was kept cold in a washtub filled with ice.

The cars parked beside and behind his van. The rest of us sat on blankets between the van and the screen. Only a few actually brought blankets; the rest of us scrounged to be the guest of one of those friends who did. Often some would end up sitting on the bare ground. I think I learned about dew at the free show.

Some of the movies I remember from the free show were Ma and Pa Kettle, Francis the Talking Mule, and an early Dean Martin and Jerry Lewis comedy.

It was a great social event, too. And educational. The first time I ever heard about marijuana was while walking back to town after the free show. Not that there was ever any marijuana use at the free show. I'm sure there wasn't. But some of the older kids did smoke tobacco cigarettes there.

Austin Briley and I were walking back with his older sister, Tessie, and her friend, Jackie Utt. Tessie and Jackie were 15 or 16; Austin and I were 10 or 11. The two girls were talking about a Canadian boy their age who was visiting his cousin in Atlanta and had been sitting on a blanket next to theirs at the movie.

"He sure is cute," Jackie said. "Do you think he will be at Crooked Creek tomorrow?" Crooked Creek was one of our two favorite swimming holes. The other was at the old Atlanta Dam.

"I don't know," Tessie answered, "but I would be careful around him. Did you see the cigarettes he was smoking?"

"I didn't notice anything other than he smoked a lot of 'em," Jackie answered. "What about them?"

"They came in a blue box. I have never seen cigarettes come in a box like that. I think they were something else." Tessie was unfamiliar with Canadian cigarette brands.

"I did see the blue box. I just thought he used the box to hide the cigarettes from his aunt and uncle." Jackie had never seen Canadian cigarettes either. "If they weren't cigarettes, what were they?"

"Mary Janes," Tessie answered.

"Mary Janes, what are those?"

"Marijuana. Sometimes they are called reefers," Tessie continued. "I read all about them last week in Look magazine. Marijuana is an illegal drug. They make cigarettes from the marijuana and sell them to teenagers. The article said that the marijuana cigarettes are called Mary Janes or reefers. They've been a problem in the big cities, even Detroit."

"Oh yeah, I've read about marijuana," Jackie said in a conspiratorial tone. "I bet that's what he was smoking."

It was Austin who brought us all back to earth. "I saw the same kind of blue boxes all over when I went with Uncle Eldon fishing in Canada last year. That kind and some others, too. Woodrow bought the blue kind just like those. Canadian cigarettes are different from ours."

"Well, maybe. He is from Canada," Jackie said. Tessie didn't say anything.

I've heard a lot about marijuana over the years since then, even defended some who were charged with marijuana offenses. But almost every time I hear someone talking about it I am reminded of that night walking home from the free show with Austin, Tessie and Jackie.

MY LIFE OF CRIME

By E. Dan Stevens (2007)

It was very short-lived. My life of crime, that is. I doubt that it would have turned out much different even if I hadn't been caught, but we'll never know. See, I was nabbed right off the bat and it scared me so much that I never wanted to risk it again.

For this story I will use first names to protect the not so innocent, and maybe not even the real first names at that.

It started out as a typical northern Michigan summer day, the year that I was ten or eleven, 1953 or 1954. Billy and I were playing in our fortress, the old well and pump structure behind my house in Atlanta. It was half-underground and had masonry walls and a concrete roof. We used an old window opening on its north side for our cannon.

The cannon was a 1946 Dodge wheel rim squeezed in the window frame. We then jammed a few bricks inside the flanges and against the frame to hold it tight. A bicycle inner tube was the propellant for the projectiles, long sticks, which we could aim through the center hole of the rim. I think we used edging strips from my dad's sawmill.

It worked pretty well, actually. Our best efforts usually propelled the stick into the alley and sometimes across to the wall of the Hogarth building, a distance of 30-40 feet from our hideout.

Another feature of our fortress was that it was dark inside. We could see out but nobody outside could see in. Nobody would know we were waiting to pounce on unsuspecting persons or vehicles traversing the alley. Actually, we only pretended to fire at real vehicles or people and would not release our missiles until after the targets had passed.

On that fateful day, Billy and I had collected our sticks and were watching out the window when a truck loaded with fruits and vegetables drove into the ally and stopped behind the hardware store next door. Because it stopped within the range of our cannon stick (did I mention before that it wasn't too accurate?), we didn't fire.

The driver went inside the hardware store, through the back door, probably to sell his produce to the employees. In those days the hardware store was also a John Deere tractor dealership and employed several people, including a full time tractor mechanic, Buster Marlatt. Buster was my sister Sally's uncle and a very close friend of my parents.

The produce truck was a small flatbed model with slatted sides. It was open in the back. While Billy and I were watching, two high school boys, John and Tom, came through the driveway alongside my house and stood at the back corner of the hardware building. They looked around but couldn't see Billy and me inside the old well house.

We watched as John and Tom walked over to the back of the truck, looked around again, and each took a cantaloupe from a crate easily within their reach. They then took off running with their plunder back through the driveway.

Nothing happened. Neither the truck's driver, still in the hardware store, nor anyone else, except us, had seen the successful theft. We sure weren't going to tell on a couple of older boys we saw nearly every day. They had gotten away with it.

"Did you see that?" I asked somewhat rhetorically. "I bet they are somewhere enjoying those cantaloupes right now."

"I really like cantaloupes," Billy said. "I wish my mother would buy them more."

We glanced at the crate of cantaloupes only fifty feet away and then at each other. "Are you thinking what I'm thinking?" I asked.

"Yeah," he answered. "We could be back in here a lot faster than it took them to get away through the driveway."

"And we only need one cantaloupe for both of us," I rationalized, "so we won't be as greedy as they were with one apiece. You stand guard by the back door and I'll snatch a melon." I was a good three inches taller than Billy.

"Okay, let's go before the driver gets back."

So off we went, clambering out the cellar-like doorway of the well house.

Billy ran to his lookout station, next to the open doorway at the back of the hardware store. In retrospect, he should have stationed himself on the far side of the door so he could have seen anyone who was approaching from inside. However, we weren't exactly experienced in that kind of thing.

I ran to the back of the truck. John and Tom had been able to simply reach into the crate and grab their booty. I quickly discovered that I was not to be so lucky. I was too short by quite a bit. There was no easy way to climb up the back of the truck so I climbed up one of the tires and then over the side rack. I landed on the truck bed okay and grabbed one of the cantaloupes.

Before I could jump down from the truck I heard Billy yell.

At the same time I heard, "Hey you. Stop!" The truck driver had Billy's arm in one hand and was looking at me. I was holding one of his cantaloupes. He had me dead to rights. I stopped.

I can't ever remember being more frightened. The man was very gruff-sounding. "I should take you to the sheriff," he said.

I think he said a lot more, but I really wasn't focusing on what he was saying. I was horrified at the prospect of him taking us back into the hardware and Uncle Buster learning what I had done.

Then it was over. He let us go, *sans* the cantaloupe, of course. Relief would be a massive understatement of my feelings at that moment.

It was a lesson well learned for me and as far as I know for Billy. I've never forgotten.

OUR FIRST PAYDAY

By E. Dan Stevens (2007)

We worked pretty hard that summer of 1960, at least for unsupervised teenagers. Bob Teets, Darrell Briley, Larry Wilson and I; we were the Can't Hardly Lumber Company. We even had a sign; it was originally made by Punk Durkee when he worked at Dad's sawmill. I don't remember whether he spelled it "Can't" as in "cannot" or "Cant" as in "cant hook." We did have a cant hook or two, but there were a few "cannots" in our operation as well.

It was quite a summer. We even had a couple of employees for a day, but that's another story. None of us had ever experienced having more than a few dollars in our pocket at any one time. That changed when we sold our first load of pulpwood.

I believe it was Chaney Fox who hauled that first load of wood to the Abitibi mill in Alpena. We were pretty proud as we watched his full double bottom truck ease up the grade to the county road.

On the other hand there was a big empty space where our wood had been stacked high before the truck came. It seemed a daunting task to cut that much wood again, and, in fact, we didn't do as well as usual for the next couple of days.

Then the check came.

It was for more money than any of us had ever had before, at least more than I'd ever had. It also looked better in total than it was going to be after divided in four.

It was probably a combination of our urge to celebrate and our reluctance to divide the check into smaller amounts that led to our decision to make a quick trip to Florida. That's right, Florida. None of us had ever been there, but it had always sounded so provocative in school and in books and in the stories told by friends who had visited there.

We left work early to cash our check before the bank closed. Bob and Darrell went to their homes to get clothes. Larry decided that if he went home he might have to stay there, so he stayed at my house.

My dad was out campaigning so I left a note and loaded a few changes of clothes (for both Larry and me) in the '37 Chevy.

While gassing up the '37 at the Shell station, I must have mentioned our plan to Al Hamilton. He was somewhere between being skeptical and thinking we were loony. Would the '37 make it there and back? Why go to Florida in the summer anyway?

Bob and Darrell arrived together and we all piled into the old Chevy and set out on our adventure.

We were about halfway between Fairview and Mio when my doubts took control. I pulled over just before the big curve and announced to the others that I was backing out. Bob must have been having similar doubts because he wanted out too.

Not so with Darrell and Larry. Before we got back to Atlanta, they had decided to continue the trip in the only other vehicle available to any of us, Darrell's homemade car.

He had built it the summer before, using a 40's Henry J frame he acquired from Abe Teets' salvage yard and a '51 Ford flathead V-8 motor and transmission. Other parts were either obtained from other junk cars, such as the axles, wheels and brakes, or individually made, such as the drive shaft. Darrell fabricated the body using shaped electrical conduit, with help from Glen Cross, plywood, an old Buick windshield, canvas and other materials. Although its lines weren't exactly sleek, it had the general shape and appearance of a sports car.

Overall it was newer than the '37 Chevy, but its durability had never really been tested. That would change.

We drove directly back to the Briley house and Darrell and Larry loaded their stuff into a space behind the seats, actually one car seat and a lawn chair, and prepared to leave. They announced that they had changed destinations and were now headed for New York City. Darrell cranked the V-8 and headed for the Shell Station to gas up.

By then it was late in the day. They drove all night, crossing into Canada at Sarnia, and arrived at Niagara Falls at daybreak.

Their only problem was at the border. The Canadian officials didn't know what to make of the car. Darrell had gotten it registered as an "assembled vehicle" with the help of an inspection report from Sam Moss, then a Deputy Sheriff, but had no other papers for the car. After some explanation by Darrell, they were allowed to proceed.

The car had run well through the night. The biggest problem was Larry's backside after sitting on the blanket-covered lawn chair which served as the passenger seat. They were beginning to be optimistic about reaching their destination as they headed east from Buffalo.

A couple of hours later their optimism began to fade as first a whining sound and then a vibration emanated from somewhere beneath them. Fortunately an exit from the turnpike was at hand, and they took it.

"It's the drive shaft," Darrell announced from beneath the car after they had stopped at the gas station by the exit. "The U-joint is shot. Needle bearings drop out every time I shake it."

It took them thirty minutes to drive to a nearby junkyard, limping along on the shoulder of the road. The bad news came quickly thereafter: no old Henry-J junkers were likely to be found anywhere in the area. They would have to refabricate the already fabricated driveshaft.

A day later they were on the road again - back to Atlanta. Their goal of reaching New York City was dashed by the costs of junkyard parts and the welding shop needed to remake the drive shaft. After also paying the motel bill and for meals they barely had enough money left to get back home.

Larry did insist on borrowing a cushion from the motel for the ride back. (They actually did return it later by mail.)

Although we had no idea when they might arrive, Bob and I and other friends kept an eye out for Darrell's car. It was almost dark on the day after they started back when we spotted it passing the Shell Station where a few of us were hanging out.

We jumped in the '37 and caught them in front of the old County Garage (now the NAPA store.) It was quite a reunion. I think we were all relieved, both them and us, that they made it back.

A day or two later we started to work again on a new pile of pulpwood, this time determined to hold onto the proceeds a little better. On the other hand, whatever we did with that next check was not nearly as memorable as what we did with the first.

APPLES, APPLES, APPLES

By E. Dan Stevens (2007)

The first thing David Wilson said to me that morning was, "You've got to come home with me after school and help clean up or I'll be grounded for a month."

My first thought was that he needed me to help with the cows. Often when we were going somewhere and we needed him to finish his chores early, I would go home with him to help in the barn. He would handle the milking machines and I would shovel; it was sort of like cleaning up, although nothing ever got really clean in the barn.

But this was different. He sounded more urgent. And he was clearly a little agitated.

So I asked, "Clean up what?"

"Apple cider." With that he walked off mumbling something about finding Punky.

It had been just over a week since David, Punky (Rod) Marlatt and I had spent a Saturday making cider with David's grandmother's cider press. We also used apples from the trees in his grandmother's back yard.

She seemed happy enough with the arrangement. At least she knew where we were. We were twelve or thirteen that fall and probably getting to the age when our parents and grandparents had reasons to worry about what we were up to.

Well, on that Saturday we were being entrepreneurs. We were making cider and we were going to sell it from my front yard in town to hunters. Small game season would be opening in two weeks, the Saturday following the Tuesday David accosted me in the hall about "cleaning up."

Actually, making cider was fun. The cider press comprised a grinder with a big handle on one end and a jack-screw press on the other. The apples were put in the top of the grinder and the ground-up pieces fell out the bottom into a several gallon stave-type bucket made of vertical wooden strips all around.

After the stave container was full of ground apples it was moved to be under the jackscrew attached to a round press that just fit inside the staves. As the press was turned, it lowered into the bucket squeezing the juice from the ground-up apples. The juice ran down a trough beneath the stave bucket into a conventional container.

The final step was to strain the juice to remove any apple pulp and seeds that might have made it through the press. We used a regular milk strainer and filters, not hard to find at his grandmother's barn, for that process.

Our genius on that particular Saturday, or at least so we thought, was to use Welch's grape juice bottles to package our product. They would be just the right size to sell at our planned stand in town, and, more significant to our effort, David's grandmother had about a dozen of them in her basement - empty and with tops.

So, after washing the grape juice bottles and letting them dry, we filled the bottles with cider and screwed on the caps. We then carried them across the road to David's house and placed them along the stairway leading to the basement.

The cider making project was not our only enterprising effort with apples during those years. A year or two later a man who sold candied apples at the fair hired us to supply him with the apples for his stand.

We supplied the first batch from one of David's grandmother's trees, but soon we had exhausted the supply from her small orchard that met his requirements. The apples needed to be sweet and ripe. Only one of her trees was ready during fair week.

Alas, finding apple trees in Montmorency County in those days was almost as easy as finding sand at Clear Lake. Although timbering was a big part of the early years of our county, there were also a large number of homesteaders who came here during the last third of the nineteenth century.

Many of the small farms and remnants of farms you see along the roads in the county now were originally homestead farms. Also, there were more than a few homestead farms which disappeared when there were no children to carry on or help work the land. Sometimes offers from timber companies were too good to resist.

One common denominator among most of the homesteaders was that they planted apple trees on their first cleared land. Whether Johnny Appleseed visited these parts, I don't know, but it is hard to find an old farm place in Montmorency County that didn't have, or in some cases still has, a small apple orchard.

So David and I had plenty of places to look for ripe eating apples for the caramel apple man. My dad's farm in Pleasant Valley had an old stand of about a dozen or so apple trees on the back part. Better was an old homestead orchard on land he owned in Vienna Township. It had some twenty trees and several produced very tasty apples.

We managed to talk one of our respective parents, I don't remember which one, in to driving us to the old orchard where we filled every bushel basket we had with great apples. The caramel apple man bought them all. I think he even had some left for his next venue. Needless to say, David and I had all the money we needed for the rides and games at the fair that year.

Oh, the apple cider project. It didn't turn out as well. I did go home with David after school that day. We both learned quite a bit about fermentation as we picked up glass and wiped cider from the steps, walls and ceiling of the basement stairway in his house.

EDGAR DOTY'S BASEBALL TEAM

By E. Dan Stevens (2007)

I was a little nervous as Mr. Doty sized me up from the top step of the dugout. After all, he was one of the most prominent businessmen in Atlanta. His wood finishing mill, hardware, cabinet shop and lumber company took up the better part of a block of the downtown. And he was the owner and manager of Atlanta's baseball team.

It was Sunday afternoon at the baseball park south of town, across from the airport. It was called Doty Field. Stacks of his lumber could be seen at his storage yard over the right field fence. Unless his team was playing out of town, there was a game at Doty Field.

"You'll do," he said. "Fifty cents for the game. If you do a good job, you can do it again next week."

I was thrilled. I was either nine or ten that summer when I worked my first baseball game for Edgar Doty. My title was "ball boy." My job was to chase down foul balls (and the occasional home run) and return the balls to the umpire. There was no throwing the balls into the crowd at those games, nor even letting a fan keep a ball he or she might catch in the bleachers. At a couple of dollars a ball, the budget didn't contemplate many lost balls.

Town baseball teams have a long tradition in Montmorency County. I have a photo of the 1903 Atlanta team. My great-uncle David

Stevens is in the picture as well as Peter Harper (my bet friend's grandfather) and the manager, Lon Manier, the only ones identified whom I knew or knew of. I have seen pictures of Hillman teams,and Lewiston teams from the same era and have heard stories of one from Rust.

In the 50's, Hillman, Lewiston and Atlanta still had teams, but the players were not always local. Some of the Atlanta regulars on Mr. Doty's team in those days were Merle Klein, Bill Gardner, Vern (Peewee) Klein, Lyle McDonnell, Doug Thompson, Red Manier and Sonny Marlatt. Along the way as they became old enough, Ron and Ray (Butch) Marlatt, Jim Briley, Gene Gerber and other good high school players made Mr. Doty's team.

Gene and Dick Sobeck were regulars from Alpena and Bobby Green and the Abbe brothers came up from Comins. During the years Lewiston didn't field a team, Joel Secrist, Doug King and others came over to play for the Atlanta team. Tom Macon came up from Detroit.

Before they went to pitch in the minor leagues, Larry and David Manier played. And there were others. I've probably forgotten as many as I remember.

My own involvement with the team expanded over the years as after a year or two of hunting down foul balls, I became the team's bat boy. Same salary, but I went along to the away games from then on.

The players were all very nice to me and I learned a lot about baseball from listening to them and Mr. Doty discussing techniques and strategy.

My personal favorite was Jim Rebennack who was the starting pitcher for many of the games from 1949 through the mid-50s. Mr. Doty gave him a job at the lumber yard during the 1949 and 1950 summers to first bring him to Atlanta. During his later years he drove up from Detroit every weekend to play ball (and to date my cousin, Mavis, whom he married in 1953.)

I remember that he and some of the other players from out of town would stop by the lumberyard gas pump after games and fill up with gas to drive back home. It was one of those where you pumped the gas up by hand to a glass cylinder at the top of the pump and then let gravity drain the tank through the hose and nozzle into the car's tank.

I talked with Jim recently about his days on the team and about Mr. Doty.

"Once," he told me, "Edgar really wanted to get a game played against Rogers City, but it had rained all day Saturday and the field was still wet. He brought in a truckload of sawdust from his planing mill, soaked it with gasoline and spread it all over the infield. He then burned it.

"It must have worked because we played the game.

"Edgar was a shrewd negotiator, too. Once the Alpena D&M team wanted us to play their home game under the lights. Since neither Atlanta nor any of the other teams had lighted fields, Edgar argued that it would be an unfair advantage for D&M. However, if they would agree to let us play David Manier, who was home on furlough, we would play under the lights. (David's professional baseball career was interrupted by his service in the Korean War.)

"They agreed. David played third base and I pitched. We won 3-0."

Atlanta played in a league with Rogers City, Cheboygan and Onaway as well as D&M and Hillman. Some years Metz, Harrisville and Lewiston also had teams. The competition was pretty even.

One year Atlanta and D&M tied for the league championship. There was no playoff, but the league did have a banquet to award trophies. That year the speaker was slated to be Dizzy Trout, a former Detroit Tigers pitcher. I wanted to go but couldn't afford the five dollar ticket.

A few days before the banquet I got word that Mr. Doty wanted to see me. I stopped by his office at the lumberyard after school. He handed me a ticket and told me that Jesse Pettijohn, a local real estate broker, had bought it for me.

Obviously, Mr. Doty had solicited it, a pretty nice way to treat his bat boy. I rode over to the banquet in Alpena with him and Mrs. Doty and had a great time. I still remember one of Dizzy Trout's jokes.*

The towns of Montmorency County have had baseball teams before and since, some of which I have no knowledge about, one of which I played on, or at least rode the bench for. But for me, baseball has never been more exciting than being the bat boy for those Edgar Doty teams.

* *The joke told by Dizzy Trout went something like this:*

"Once when I was in the minor leagues, the team scout asked me to go look at a young prospect who was pitching his last high school game that night. He was a dandy. He struck out the first twenty-six batters and the twenty-seventh batter hit a foul popup to the first baseman for the last out.

"The next day I reported back to the scout and told him what had hap-

pened.

     'Did you get his name?' he asked.

     'I thought you knew his name,' I answered.

     'Oh, we knew about the pitcher,' he responded, 'but we want to sign the kid who hit the foul ball.'"

DEER SEASON

By E. Dan Stevens (2007)

"Is that a deer in the road?"

I looked up the hill ahead to where Bob Teets was pointing. "It sure is," I answered.

We were in the '37 Chevrolet, just passing Jim Kent's house, heading west on M-32 on our way to my dad's hunting land on Camp 8 Road. It was about 10:00 a.m. on the third day of deer season, 1959, my first day hunting that year.

As we got closer, the deer crossed the road, heading north, up the steep bank where the road was cut through the side of a hill. A gentle slope to a small field, Les Schmier's garden in the summer, bordered the south side of M-32, but the deer clearly didn't want to go back that way. Probably spooked by some hunters in the woods behind the field, we reasoned.

We could see that the deer couldn't get over the fence at the top of the road bank. It was steep and a few inches of snow remained on the ground from the storm two days before the season. That would have been the 13th, a Friday as I recall. Each time the deer tried to jump the fence, its feet would slip down the bank.

We were almost even with the deer when we saw the horns.

"It's a buck!" we exclaimed, almost simultaneously.

I stopped the car and slowly opened my door. Bob would have spooked the deer from his side. He took his gun out of its case and handed it to me along with a couple of shells as I crouched beside the car.

One might ask why it was mid-morning on the third day of season, and I was just heading to the woods for the first time. The reason was that like many of my schoolmates I had been working twelve hour shifts since two or three days before season. I worked for Al Hamilton and George Pinchock at the Shell Station, 8:00 p.m. to 8:00 a.m. The Shell Station was one of two businesses in Atlanta, Michigan, to stay open around the clock for the few days before and the first three days of deer season. The other was the Mason and Mills Gulf Station.

The dates were the same as now, November 15th through the 30th, but the deer season was bigger somehow, more of an event which had no equal throughout the year. There was no school for the first week, not so much for us to hunt, although a lot of us (and teachers) did, but because the businesses in town needed extra help during that week. It was a great time to earn Christmas money.

During those first few days of season, parked cars lined not only the main street through the business district, but the side streets as well. I can remember cars parked along M-33 as far north as Hay Meadow Creek.

Hunters would flock to town at night, checking out the buck pole in front of Tunnicliff's Drug Store, buying ammunition from Erity's Sports Shop, eating at Utt's Cafe or Gavine's Cafe or Goldie's Grill or the Hotel. They bought supplies at McMurphy's IGA or Peterson's General Store or Ferguson's or Wilson's or Reiman's. A few might even go to one of the bars - Benson's, Wedge Inn (later Walker's) or Claude Mowery's Hotel - well, maybe more than a few.

Once when I was ten or eleven, I was carrying groceries for my mother from Peterson's when the door to Wedge's Inn burst open in front of me and two men came out, hunting knives in hand, circling each other and threatening to strike. I stopped, of course, heart in my throat.

I'll never know how serious the knife-fighting hunters were because before they could do more than make a few feints at each other, a two-tone green Chrysler pulled up and stopped in the middle of the street. Out stepped Sheriff Charles Brown. Though not large in stature, Sheriff Brown was carrying a sawed-off shotgun and looked every bit ready to use it if necessary. Within seconds the would-be knife-fighters were in the back seat of the Chrysler. They didn't look very tough anymore as they answered questions for the sheriff.

I remembered the ice cream I was carrying and hurried on home.

Many of the families in Atlanta with extra rooms rented them to hunters in those days. My parents did. Two of the couples who stayed at our house came back year after year. One was from what is now Westland and the other from Ohio. Even before I was old enough to hunt, I made a few extra quarters "guiding" our renters.

Once I had shown one of the ladies where to sit on a deer trail near an old apple orchard and then took her husband to another place. On my way out I saw the lady walking around in a circle so I went over to see if anything was wrong. She told me that a large buck had walked right in front of her and she had been so mesmerized that she forgot she had a gun and was supposed to shoot the deer until it was out of sight. Buck fever, we called it.

Hunting seemed a lot different then and not just because the hunters wore red clothing, instead of today's hunter orange, and were required to display deer licenses on their backs like a car tag. Baiting and bait piles were unheard of and almost no one hunted from a blind. The good hunters were those who could locate a good spot along a deer trail and had the patience to wait. We would usually sit if possible. In fact having a good stump to sit on or a tree as a backrest were important aspects of a good hunting spot.

There were also some pretty good stalkers back then. Of course the stalkers helped the sitters by causing the deer to move.

And then there were we lucky ones who came across a buck on their way to the woods in the middle of the morning on the third day of season. While I was loading Bob's gun, the buck gave up on getting across the fence and ran back down to Les Schmier's field. It was still reluctant to go back in the woods behind the field and stopped just short of the trees.

Bob's gun had a peep sight, a novelty for me. It was my first buck. We were back in town before noon showing it off.

SLEDDING

By E. Dan Stevens (2008)

During the fifties when the first snow came each year we thought first about keeping the skating area on the dam pond clear - and then about other winter activities that sort of took over as the snow got deeper and skating became more difficult. Some skied on weekends over at Sheridan Valley. Some used snowshoes to rabbit hunt or get into the woods when the snow got really deep or just for fun. Some had ice shanties and went fishing. However, almost all of us growing up in Atlanta, Michigan, in those days were into sledding.

Next to ice skates, our most cherished Christmas gift in those days was a new sled, at least a new one to us. My first flyer sled was used. I got it when I was nine and it lasted until I had graduated from high school and moved on. Although they were made by several companies, the American Flyer and Flexible Flyer were the brands I remember, hence the sometimes reference to them as "flyer" sleds. And they could fly, too, with the right kind of snow conditions.

Sledding and tobogganing were pretty big deals for children of all ages. In Atlanta we had the Hill. The Big Rock kids had Mount Vernon. The coming of snowmobiles was still many years in the future.

We didn't have dishes, plastic sleds or any other kinds of sledding devices in those days other than the flyer-type sleds and toboggans. Oh, I did have a bobsled that was given to me by my brother-in-law, but I only used it a couple of times. (It was involved in an incident where I thought I was a goner, but that's another tale.)

The flyer sleds had a slatted wood deck mounted about five inches above steel runners. A wooden crossbar near the front of the sled was used to steer the sled by twisting the forward part of the runners in one direction or the other. The sleds came in varying lengths, most commonly between three and five feet. One or more riders could sit on the sled, steering with the front rider's feet and a rope tied to the opposite ends of the steering bar. Alternatively, one rider could lie on the sled, stomach down, face forward, and steer with his or her hands.

The sleds wouldn't work very well in deep or unpacked snow. They needed ice or packed snow. After a new snow of any significant amount, we would have to pack the snow on the sledding run, usually by tramping it down with our feet until a sled could go down. After that first sled went down, we finished packing it with our sleds. After each trip the run would get faster as the packed snow became harder and the half-inch wide sled runners dug in less.

Toboggans generally needed less snow prep for a successful run. A toboggan is a wooden sled with a curved front. The entire wooden floor of the toboggan rides on the snow. Most toboggans were built for multiple riders. The front rider, often the smallest, would be on his or her knees or have legs bunched under the curled front. The other riders would sit on the deck with their legs and arms wrapped around the person ahead. Turning was a team effort - lean left, lean right.

The Hill was on the north edge of Atlanta, across M-33 from Wilson's Grocery, between the Davis' and Chadwick's houses. It had two runs: one was pretty much for toboggans, and the other we packed down more for sleds. The toboggan run was no picnic. It was bumpy and there were trees and bushes pretty close on each side. The sled run ended in Merve and Helen Davis' front yard. They were kind enough to put a gate in their back fence and leave it open during sledding season.

The sledding run had two starting levels: the top and a small level spot about halfway down. The level spot acted as a jump for those brave enough to start from the top. You could really fly from up there. Sleds could be steered quite a bit, a necessity because after you came over the jump you had to maneuver through the Davis fence gate and then slide sideways to a stop in their yard. The alternative was to continue down their driveway and on to M-33. On good sledding Saturdays there might be twenty or thirty of us pulling our sleds up to one of the starting levels, waiting our turn, and then flying down the Hill. During my younger years I was quite content to start my runs from the first level. We had to be careful, though, to be sure we wouldn't get run over by the older boys who started from the top. I can vividly remember watching in awe as they came streaking down, often becoming airborne as they went over the level area where I was standing. Bob Paul, Donny Dice, Foster Cameron and Ed Manier come to mind.

A few years later it was Harry Dice, Larry Wilson, Austin Briley, me and others coming from the top and yelling for the younger kids to stay out of our path. The girls, too: Karen Davis (it was her yard), Mary Lou Paul, Mary Ann Blamer, Jennie Benson, Claudia Cameron, my cousin Sylvia, and many others were regulars at the Hill.

Mount Vernon was the site of an accident that laid up Jim Briley for several weeks during his early teens with a broken leg. It was the highest hill on the back of the old Meyer place, about a mile west of the old Big Rock Store. Sledders reached it (on foot) from Manier Road.

Jim's mishap occurred at an outing put on by the Big Rock Church youth group - tobogganing at Mount Vernon. Jim was in the front of the toboggan, the youngest and smallest. His older sister Marlene, Joan Basch, Bill Harrison and Mary LaRue Manier were on behind him. Down the hill they went, spraying the new snow, gathering speed as they neared the bottom. They didn't see the old fencepost in the dark until it was too late to turn.

Sonny Marlatt told me about it. "Jim was the only one seriously hurt. His leg was pretty messed up. We got him on another toboggan and pulled him through the deep snow back to Manier Road. The Basches had a Nash automobile with a reclining seat. We got Jim in the car and took him to the Alpena Hospital."

We're probably lucky that more of us sledders didn't end up like Jim. Flying down the Hill, head first, and through the gate at the bottom didn't leave much room for error. But the thrill - well, it was fun, really fun!

THE BOBSLED

By E. Dan Stevens (2008)

"This thing sure is heavy," Larry Wilson said as we rested at the first level, halfway up the hill behind the Davis' house.

"Maybe we ought to try it from here first," chimed in Harry Dice as we all tried to catch our breath.

"Naw, let's go from the top." Austin Briley was always just a little more of a daredevil than the rest of us.

The four of us had just pulled and pushed my bobsled up to the first starting level of Atlanta's sledding hill. It didn't look much like the bobsleds you see in the Olympics, and I actually only used it a few times, but I was the proud owner of that bobsled from the time I was nine years old until - well, I don't exactly remember what happened to it or when. I probably gave it to some unsuspecting kid when I left to go to college, just as my then soon to be brother-in-law, Gary Whitehead, gave it to me when he left for college in 1952.

As I said, it wasn't very fancy. Gary built it himself, and it was heavy. It comprised a deck about two feet wide by six feet long, constructed with two by sixes atop two small sleighs, also constructed from two by sixes, with strap iron attached for runners. A steering wheel on a shaft and a spool and rope apparatus, similar to the mechanism used in outboard boats back then, provided the steering. The sled itself was much like a smaller version of the old logging sleighs used by the early white pine lumberjacks. My dad always referred to those rigs as a "set of sleighs."

One feature of a set of sleighs, and the bobsled, was that a chain from the rear of the left runner of the front sleigh was attached to the front of the right runner of the rear sleigh, and another chain attached between the other runners in like fashion. The chains formed a cross between the two sleighs. In this manner when the front sleigh turned to the right the rear sleigh would be caused by the chains to turn left and vice versa. The result was that the back sleigh would follow the front around a curve rather than the whole thing sliding one way or the other.

For years the bobsled collected dust in a corner of the old garage behind my house. When we were younger some of my friends and I would sit on it and pretend to be flying down a bobsled run, turning the wheel back and forth as the course required. Once we even broke the steering rope as we pulled too hard on the steering wheel against the sleighs which were immovable on the concrete floor.

However, it wasn't until that day when I was a teenager that we actually used the bobsled on snow. Harry and Austin had helped me pull the bobsled from my garage to the sledding hill. The three of us and Larry had muscled it up to the first starting level.

Austin was outvoted so we lined it up at the first level for our first run. The four of us piled on and headed down. We nearly missed the gate opening, the bobsled steering much more erratically than I had anticipated, but we did get it stopped in the Davis' yard. It didn't have brakes; we used our feet.

We started the second run a little higher up the hill, but not all the way from the top. This time either Harry or Larry steered, I don't remember which. We were taking turns. The bobsled was going a lot faster when we passed through the gate, and none of us were disposed to try to brake with our feet at that speed. Zoom, right through the Davis' yard, down their driveway and across M-33.

I guess if a car had been coming it wouldn't have ended so well. As it happened, we plowed into the snow-bank on the other side of the road and stopped without much damage.

That was its last run down the hill. At the end of the day a couple of us hauled it back to my garage.

We did use it one more time, though. In those days before snow-mobiles and road salt, we sometimes defied good sense (and probably our parents' rules) by pulling sleds and toboggans behind cars on some of the back roads. We were usually pretty careful, but I can remember one instance when a girl fell off the lead toboggan and was run over by the one behind. Luckily she suffered only a few minor abrasions from the accident.

Someone came up with the idea of having Bob Miller pull my bobsled behind his car one winter night. Bob was a really nice guy who had just moved to Atlanta from "down below" (a phrase we used to describe all of Michigan south of Standish.) And he had a car, a 1950 Chevrolet. We knew he didn't have any experience pulling sleds, so we talked to him about the most obvious danger, stopping faster than the sled could stop.

We headed south from town and then east on Airport Road. Four or five of us were on the bobsled. I was steering. Then Bob started to turn right on South Airport road. He was going way too fast. I suddenly realized that we had forgotten to tell him about whiplash.

I can still remember the sensation as we swung around on the end of the rope as the car turned, helplessly propelled like a shot at the end of a sling toward the big snow-bank at the east side of the intersection. The biggest problem was the stop sign and its steel post. I couldn't tell if we were going to hit it or not.

My first sensation after the impact was wondering whether the whiteness all around me meant that I was in heaven. Then I recognized one of the voices I was hearing. Mary Ann Blamer was telling someone that she could see a boot.

We had missed the sign but still hit the snowbank pretty hard. It took a few minutes for us all to be extricated from the snow. The chains and steering ropes were broken on the bobsled so we left it there.

A few days later a couple of us borrowed the Shell Station's pickup and hauled the bobsled back to my garage. That was the last time we ever tried to use it.

SHERIDAN VALLEY

By E. Dan Stevens (2008)

I don't know if I can adequately express in words what a great thing the Sheridan Valley Ski Hill was for those of us who grew up in Atlanta and Lewiston - and also for our children. Well, not always for me. The last time I came down the hill I didn't make it all the way standing up. For the last part I was on my back on the meat wagon toboggan cushioning a broken ankle and holding one and a half skis.

Nevertheless, most of my memories of the Sheridan Valley Ski Hill are much better than that one. It's where I learned to ski when I was nine and for the next several years spent quite a few Saturdays or Sundays or both skiing. It often depended on who we could catch a ride with. Sometimes it was Marion or Loren Briley, sometimes Mrs. Durkee or my mother or someone's older brother or sister.

I was never a very good skier and probably spent as much time by the fire in the warming cabin as on the slopes. Still, I was around a lot of good skiers and enjoyed trying to keep up. Darrell Briley was the best in my age group from Atlanta. I also got to know Linda Neuenfelt, Doug Mowery and Eddie Boetcher from Lewiston and Dick Scarsella from Loud at the ski hill several years before they became my classmates in high school. They formed the nucleus of a very good high school ski team, one of many over the years coached by Joe Peck. At least two Atlanta High skiers went on to compete in college, Betsy Halberg at Michigan State in the early 50's and North Shetter at Middlebury College in the mid 60's.

My first skiing heroes were some of the older Lewiston guys when I was first learning at Sheridan Valley. I can still see Tom May, Leroy Allen and Tom Halberg charging down the hill and whipping through the gates during the frequent racing events held at the ski hill many Saturdays.

It's hard to be from Atlanta in those days and talk about skiing without mentioning Joe Peck, then the high school principal. He was an avid skier and was at Sheridan Valley almost every weekend day it was open. He taught me the basics of skiing the first time I went at age nine. He also arranged for a bus to take Atlanta students to the hill one afternoon a week during ski season and was the ski team coach.

He even built and operated a small hill just west of Atlanta to teach beginners skiing fundamentals. We affectionately called it Peck's Peak. Until just a few years ago one or two of the old poles with car rims atop for the tow-rope apparatus he constructed still were evident alongside M-32 just west of the former Atlanta Excavating garage.

The Sheridan Valley Ski Hill was a labor of love started by the Lewiston Boosters. It operated from the late 40's until the mid-90's. Hundreds of volunteers over the years built, operated and maintained the hill and ski facilities.

The original ski runs were cleared by hand with bushmans, cross-cuts and axes. The stumps were dug with shovels and pickaxes. Dynamite was used to break up some of the larger ones, but the final removal was by hand labor.

"I helped my dad and some of the other men. I was just a boy then," Bruce Huston told me. "Toward the end of the clearing process a guy who lived near the ski hill showed up with a chain saw, the first one I ever saw. His name was Carl Gould, but went by his nickname, Moose Ears. He was a welcome sight for the rest of us. Not only did he do most of the cutting after that, but he told great stories, most of them tall-tales."

When the original clubhouse burned, it was replaced with mostly volunteer labor. Hank Halberg designed and built the huge fireplace in the center of the new building. Hank had also helped build the original rope tows and was one of two people at the hill who could splice a broken ski rope. He also cleared and built Hank's Hollow, a back run enjoyed by many of us over the years.

I don't have a complete list of those who made Sheridan Valley work so well for so many years, but Carl Allen and Gordon Huston were two of the founders. Others who played significant roles during the early years were May and Osmo Pynnonen, Cecilia and Bugs May, Hank and

Grace Halberg, Ida and Buck Rinke, Bruce and Marian Huston, Edith Barstow and, of course, Joe and Shirley Peck.

In a recent conversation, Grace Halberg told me, "The ski hill was a project of the whole town. Many of the ideas came from Nina Buell and Mickey Huston, and the rest of us carried them out. Hank was there most of the time it was open, and many of the ladies, me included, ran the snack bar.

"There were many good times involved, lots of camaraderie," she continued. "We went with our children on many occasions to racing events at other ski hills in northern Michigan. Once I remember several of us parents and the skiers staying in an old bunkhouse near Cadillac. We only had a fireplace for heat and it got really cold.

"And we had the pleasure of seeing our son, Tom, and Tom May being selected for a team representing the central United States to compete in a national ski competition in Reno. They met the other team members in Cadillac and went by bus to Chicago where they caught a train to Reno. All because of Sheridan Valley."

Over the years sons and daughters and new volunteers kept the program going. Bruce and Marion Huston, Tom May, Jerry Skog, Toy and Esther Qujala, Bob Stevenson, Leo Shuster, George and Mary Ann Mays are just the ones I have been made aware of. I have been assured that there were many, many others.

My personal experience with the ski hill did not end with my broken ski and broken ankle, although I never again bought a pair of skis or went downhill skiing. (One of the immediate reasons then was that Coach McDonnell didn't like basketball players skiing. One could ask Larry Wilson for more details about that rule.) I watched both of my children learn to ski at Sheridan Valley under the tutelage of Jerry Peck and Mark Huston and others continuing the Sheridan Valley tradition of volunteer instructors for new skiers. The main tow had upgraded to a T-Bar by then. Skiing has been a passion for both of them ever since.

"It was natural that my generation took over Sheridan Valley from our parents, and then our children, too," said Bruce Huston. "Even when it was no longer feasible to operate and we had to disband, its assets were distributed to community causes. Programs at the Atlanta and Lewiston schools, the Lewiston Library, and the curling club youth program were some that come to mind.

"But I can't let you go without telling one story about Joe Peck," he continued. "Joe played such a big role at Sheridan Valley over the years, but when he first came to Michigan from Arkansas in 1950, or so, he had never skied. My dad, not the best skier himself, was leading Joe down the back trail at the hill on his first run. Joe, being much heavier, was overtaking Dad and asked how he was supposed to stop. Dad told him to grab a tree. Joe did and ended up carrying the broken-off tree with him all the way down the hill."

Unfortunately the ski hill has closed. At least one person has stepped into the void for Atlanta school students. Chuck Sanglier, a Sheridan Valley veteran from Lewiston and now an Atlanta school bus driver, carries on the tradition as advisor to the ski club. He takes students over to Treetop every week just as Joe Peck used to do for us fifty years ago at Sheridan Valley. He even has a store of ski equipment that he provides for the young skiers at no charge. The Sheridan Valley founders would be proud.

ATLANTA'S HOCKEY TEAM

By E. Dan Stevens (2008)

We had just finished a round of golf last summer and were enjoying some refreshments with the other golfers when I asked Vernon Klein whether he and his friends had ever played hockey while growing up in Atlanta. I asked because when I came along some fifteen years later, we didn't very much and when we did attempt to play down on the river we just used some old scrap lumber, not real sticks, and an old tape-wrapped baseball for a puck. On the other hand, the Sport Shop in town had some old hockey sticks next to the baseball bats, but I never saw anyone buy or use one.

His answer surprised me. "Yes, oh yes!" he exclaimed. "We had a team. Your cousin, George, was one of the stars."

It was news to me. Since then I have talked to several people who remember Atlanta's hockey team and one other team member, Mike Davis.

"It was started by Pat Hart, the town barber. He was from Canada and was ardent about hockey. I think the team lasted three years. We got to be pretty good," Vernon continued. "We played teams from Alpena, Cheboygan, and Petoskey. And maybe some other towns. The last year we beat them all.

"It was in the late 30's and early 40's, before the war. In fact, I think the war ended it. Most of us were twelve, thirteen or fourteen, just before high school.

"That first year we built a rink on the vacant lot across the street from the school, west, and just east of the road commission garage. It didn't work out all that well. The board around the ice was only about a foot high, and we had to spend a lot of time chasing down pucks outside the rink. And, of course, each time the puck went out we had to stop play and have a new face-off. We only played Alpena that first year.

"By the second year they had constructed a new rink down at the park, about where the pavilion is now. It had much taller boards, five feet or so. It also had lights and a warming shanty. Mr. Cauchon, I remember, worked for the Township and kept the fire going for us in the shanty. He also watered the ice every night after we left to make new ice. It seems like there was recreational skating lots of evenings, too.

"We had a lot of good players, not just George. Quite a few that I can remember," Vernon continued. "Glen Mowery was one of our stars, too. Orlaf McKenzie, Royce Bowman, Ed Secrist, Boyden Davis, Dick Mowery, Floyd Willis, Elwin (Red) Manier, Vernon Secrist, Joe Cauchon and Mike Davis played. There were probably some others I can't think of.

"I was one of the younger ones, but we had some really good skaters and Mr. Hart was pretty good at teaching us the skills and strategy of hockey. His wife, Maude, was around a lot, too. She was also Canadian and knew the game.

"One time Mr. Hart was telling our goalie, Red Manier, to ignore the shots that were high or wide of the net. 'Let 'em go, let 'em go!' he yelled. Red let the next high shot go as instructed. Unfortunately Mr. Hart was standing right behind the net while he coached and the puck hit him. He didn't tell Red to 'let 'em go' after that, at least while he was anywhere near the goal.

"Another time we all got a scare when two of our players collided during a practice session. Royce Bowman and Orlaf McKenzie were both skating hard and watching the puck when they
met head-on at mid-ice. No such thing as helmets for hockey in those days. Down they went. Royce was slow getting up and Orlaf didn't get up at all for a while. He had a bad concussion and remained out of commission for a several days."

It took Mike Davis a few seconds to focus back to those days when I asked him about the hockey team. "I haven't thought about that for years," he said. "But, yeah, my brother Boyden and I played."

He remembered many of the same things about the two rinks and the other players as Vernon had related. He laughed when he thought about Pat Hart. "He was a big man, hadn't missed too many meals along the way. One time he fell on the ice and couldn't get up. Fortunately it was that first year when we had the small sideboards. We players had to slide him over to the edge of the ice so we could put his feet over the side to help him stand.

"But he got us in shape, worked us hard. I remember skating around and around the rink until I was ready to drop. Even though we weren't as good that first year as most of the other teams we played, we could usually out-skate them.

"Coach Hart was pretty innovative when it came to equipment, too. We were all poor as church mice, and what he couldn't scrounge for us we didn't have. Our shin pads were made of cardboard folded under our socks. Sometimes we used cardboard to protect other places as well."

The team also had a fan base. Last summer I mentioned to Doreen (Stevens) Moreau and Mary Elinor (Cameron) Cauchon that Vernon had told me about the hockey team. Although professing to have been very, very young girls at the time, they both cheerfully recounted running down to the park after school to watch the boys practice and going to the games on Saturdays.

"I think we won all our games that last year," Vernon recalled, "although I can't be sure about Cheboygan. One time we went up there and they didn't have all their players. So they used two independent league players (adults) as defensemen. Even though they weren't allowed to skate on offense out of their defensive zone, they were still pretty tough on us when we skated into their zone on offense.

"All in all, though, we made a pretty good showing for ourselves. Pat Hart brought us from a bunch of farm and small-town boys with no experience into a team that beat all comers from the larger towns around us in just three years. We were all quite proud to be the Atlanta Hockey Team."

IT'S NOT LOADED

By E. Dan Stevens (2008)

It was spring, or at least the time for spring. The snow was mostly gone. We were thirteen or fourteen, my buddy and I, not yet dating girls, but starting to appreciate them for more than just their abilities to hunt and fish and play marbles. Roberta had moved to Atlanta a few months before with her mother and little brother. Her father was in the military, stationed in Germany or some other overseas post. They moved away after that school year, to where I don't know.

She was in my class and was one of those girls who could be appreciated for reasons over and above her fishing skills, if in fact she had any. She lived in a house on the highway just east of Atlanta, on the southern shore of Twin Lake, well, almost. Haymeadow Creek and the railroad grade were between her house and the lake.

My friend and I were in the field behind the Pettinger's house when we decided to walk down the railroad grade to Twin Lake. It was a Saturday, a pretty nice day, sun shining and not too cold. We looked for railroad spikes among the old cross ties, deer tracks in the adjoining cedar swamp, and signs of trout in the creek that paralleled the grade as we moseyed eastward. We were probably also having a major philosophical discussion, such as why girls were looking better this year than last or something like that.

Soon we were at Twin Lake. We looked out across to the eastern and northern shorelines and the bare popular trees growing on the slopes rising away from the lake. It was just a lake, too early to fish.

Alas, on the other side of the grade was something far more interesting, Roberta's house. A walking bridge crossed the creek connecting
the old grade to the yard. We crossed it. I don't remember if Roberta's
house had been our destination all along or whether we just decided that
since we were there we would stop by, but either would have been plausi-
ble. In those days it was perfectly acceptable to visit anyone in town unan-
nounced, especially for us kids.

Roberta's mother answered the door. She seemed pleased to see us,
invited us in and called Roberta. Roberta came into the kitchen and
appeared happy with our visit as well, so we took off our jackets and
accepted her mother's offer of freshly baked cookies.

The cookies were good. Roberta suggested a board game, Monop-
oly I think, which sounded okay to us. We might even be offered some
more cookies. For the next hour, or so, we played the game. Roberta's
mother played too.

During all of this time Roberta's little brother, probably five or six,
was running around the house, occasionally playing with his toys, but
mostly vying for attention from his mother and us three older children
who were immersed in our game. He wasn't exactly being a pest, but he
was distracting at the very least.

At some point the conversation switched to Roberta's absent father
and his military exploits. Roberta asked us if we wanted to see his World
War II pistol, a Colt .45 automatic. We said, "Sure." She turned to her
mother, who nodded, and then went to a dresser to get the gun.

"It's not loaded," she said. "Dad wouldn't let us keep a loaded gun
in the house."

Other than a .22 caliber target pistol Jim Durkee's older brother
owned, I had never seen a real handgun up close. My dad didn't own one.
My friend, on the other hand, was familiar with the Colt .45 automatic
pistol because his father had also brought one back from his service in
World War II.

Roberta handed me the gun, once again assuring me, "It isn't
loaded."

I looked it over. I remember being surprised at how heavy it was,
but I didn't have a clue as to how it worked. Well, I did know what the
trigger was for; I had hunted since I was old enough to carry a gun, but I
didn't know how to cock it, where the safety was or how it was loaded.

After I had looked it over, I handed the gun to my buddy. He did
know quite a bit about it and while examining it he pulled the slide back

to cock the gun. He looked in the chamber and didn't see a bullet. After a few minutes, we were ready to give the gun back to Roberta's mother to put away. My friend couldn't figure out how to get the gun un-cocked without pulling the trigger, so he pulled the trigger.

At this point I should explain a little about growing up in Montmorency County back then and guns. Our dads all hunted and so did we as soon as we were able. We were taught with rifles and shotguns, but the lessons applied to all guns. You never pointed a gun, loaded or unloaded, at a person, yourself included, or at anything else you didn't plan to shoot. I remember that my dad had taken my .22 rifle away on one of my first hunting excursions because I was careless about where I allowed the gun to be pointed. I was embarrassed at the time, but I was never careless about pointing a gun ever again.

My friend, no doubt, had the same gun safety training from his father. Good thing. When he pulled the trigger on Roberta's father's gun to un-cock it, their television set exploded. Somehow the gun was loaded.

We all sat there stunned for what seemed like a long time, but was probably only seconds. Roberta's mother broke the silence, "He always assured me it wasn't loaded." She then turned to us and said, "It wasn't your fault, but I think you two should leave now."

We did. Walking back along the railroad grade, both still pretty shaky, he told me, "Her brother was such a little brat that I could have pointed at him when I pulled that trigger, just to pretend, you know. I'm glad I knew better."

4TH GRADE IN HILLMAN

By E. Dan Stevens (2008)

Not many people know that I attended the fourth grade in Hillman. Fact is there are probably a few people around, those my age with memories still intact, who would swear they remember sitting with me in Mrs. Walker's fourth grade classroom in Atlanta. Actually, my fourth grade experiences in Hillman occurred while I was in the fifth grade in Atlanta.

If you have stayed with me this far and are a little confused, I will try to explain. You see, my mother taught the fourth grade in Hillman the year I was in the fifth grade in Atlanta (1953-1954) and on some of Atlanta's vacation days I went with her to school in Hillman.

For those who never knew her, my mother, Rose Stevens, was a transplant to northern Michigan. She was born and raised in North Carolina and met and married my father there. To the best of my knowledge she was very content to be the wife of a college professor and (later) executive for the North Carolina Wildlife Federation. Family friends included the Governor and other government officials as well as college faculty and their spouses. Mother was active in several women's organizations including the venerable Raleigh Book Club.

If she ever complained or objected when Dad wanted to move us back to his home town of Atlanta, Michigan, population three hundred and light-years away from the life she was familiar with, I never knew.

Here, she taught in public schools for almost twenty years, was active in many groups, including being a charter member of the Friends of the Library, and was a spirited member of the Atlanta Congregational Church. But she never lost her southern accent.

Mother's first Michigan teaching job was in Hillman. As I said, she taught the fourth grade. During that first year, the Hillman elementary school did not have the first week of deer season off, but my school in Atlanta did. Consequently, I went to school with her for at least three days that week.

The Hillman School was in the old red brick schoolhouse downtown, west of Main Street. It housed grades kindergarten through twelve and also the county normal school. The building was later purchased and used by Wayne Wire Corporation.

The first day there I spent in her fourth grade classroom. About the only things I remember from that day were recess and a couple of the girls, Rosie Guy and Jane Smart.

Recess was memorable because the fifth grade participated at the same time and, like fifth-graders in Atlanta, football was the recess sport *de jour* during the fall months. At the Atlanta school, however, the teachers would only allow us to play "touch" football, no tackling allowed. Hillman didn't have that rule.

Since I was visiting the fourth grade, I played on the fourth grade against the fifth grade at that first recess. On the first play they gave me the ball and I ran around the right end. That's when I learned we were playing "tackle." BAM! I believe it was Nelson Farrier. Down I went. Did I tell you that the Hillman elementary school playground was rocky? It was.

At that recess I met for the first time some of the Hillman guys I would compete with for many years after in junior high and then high school on the basketball court and football and baseball fields. In addition to Nelson, Charlie Powell, Bob Hunt and Jim Oswald come to mind.

They were all very nice to me, being from Atlanta and all. In fact, they invited me to attend their fifth grade class, much more to my liking, for the next day. I did. Incidentally, tackle football was a lot more fun when playing with the fifth grade against the fourth than vice-versa.

A couple of postscripts to this story: First, my mother moved on from the Hillman elementary school to teach English, her college major, at Onaway High School. In those days the portion of M-33 from Canada Creek Ranch to Onaway was a rough, narrow road with several ninety-degree turns and almost no shoulder. Not much traffic either. During the winter months she carried survival supplies in the car trunk: a shovel, some sand, food and a warm sleeping bag. Fortunately, she never had to use them.

After several years at Onaway, Mother was offered a position in Atlanta, teaching kindergarten in the morning, then serving as school librarian in the afternoon. Even though the assignment was not as much to her liking initially, the convenience was compelling. She continued at the Atlanta school until her death in 1969.

More than a few times in my life I have benefitted from experiences with my mother's former students from both Hillman and Onaway whose interactions with me were enhanced by their regard for her.

Secondly, my warm feelings toward the Hillman guys and gals have continued to evolve from those fourth grade visits at their school. I remember running into Jim Oswald at a Detroit area wedding a few years after high school. Old home week. During the late 60's and early 70's when my work took me to Marquette a couple of times a year, Dick Coombs' apartment was my home away from home.

I have even been an admirer of Hillman High School sports successes, except, of course, when Atlanta was the opponent. Even though those guys I originally met when I visited their fourth grade were a pretty good match later for us Atlanta guys on the court and football field and diamond, our games were fun and mostly friendly. One exception: I've never forgiven Joe Konwinski, coming in to pitch to me with the bases loaded and two out in the ninth, for striking me out on three pitches.

CANOE RACES

By E. Dan Stevens (2008)

It was the Fourth of July weekend, probably 1953. Darrell Briley and I were sitting on the top diving limb of the giant old willow tree at the Atlanta Dam. We had climbed out to nearly the end, one of us on each side of an upright branch which we held to keep from falling the ten or fifteen feet to the water below. Our eyes were glued to the place where the Thunder Bay River came into view to the west where it rounded the south end of the island.

"They should be coming soon," he said as he continued to gaze upriver. He was excited because his brother, Dennis, and partner, Terry Brooks, were competing in the annual Atlanta Canoe Race. Although barely teenagers, they were very competitive with all of the paddlers, including the adults.

The canoe race was one of many activities held in Atlanta as part of the 4th of July celebration each year, often on the 3rd, but sometimes on the 4th, depending on the days of the week the annual celebration covered. In those days the festivities lasted for three or four days. The bingo tent, at least one baseball game, the parade, fireworks, games and activities in the park, and the canoe race, all features of the holiday, were held over those few days to commemorate our nation's birth.

The canoe racers started at the dam and paddled upriver to Lake Fifteen. There they circled the lake three times and then returned down river to the dam, the finish line.

Spectators crowded the dam to watch the start as the canoes lined along the dam, sterns to the concrete wall which faced upriver before the dame was rebuilt in the early 70's. After the canoes disappeared around the island, many of the spectators jumped in their cars and drove to the Lake Fifteen campground to watch as the racers circled the lake, and then returned to the dam to see the finish.

The Atlanta race was one of many in the area during those days. An even larger race was the annual Hillman to Alpena competition along the Thunder Bay River. The AuSable River Marathon, was, and still is, the main event. Many of the major races then were international events, drawing contestants from not only Michigan and Wisconsin, but several also from Canada.

However, some of the best paddlers were homegrown. Jack Kent and Merle Klein were successful here and also on the AuSable and other prestigious race events. Glen and Ralph Cross were very good as were other Montmorency based adult racers.

"Here they come!" Darrell exclaimed.

Sure enough, a single canoe came into view as it rounded the point, probably Klein and Kent, we thought. That canoe was half-way to the dam when the next canoes came into sight, a cluster of four. As they got closer we could see that Terry and Dennis were in that second group.

I think it was at that moment that Darrell and I decided to follow in his brother's and Terry's footsteps and become canoe racers. We had been watching them practice nearly every day for the past year. They would meet in the early evening at the canoe behind Dennis' house, pick it up and carry it on the run the hundred feet, or so, to the river, drop it in and jump in, still on the run, and paddle hard for the next hour or two, Terry in the front, Dennis in the back.

And all that practice paid off. They almost always won in their junior age class and more often than not competed well against the seniors. When canoe racing enthusiasts from Oscoda County established a Michigan Junior Championship Event over a twenty-five mile stretch of the AuSable River, it was probably because they had some very fine junior racers in Mio and they wanted to crown them with the state junior title. Didn't work. For all three years of their eligibility, Terry and Dennis won the race and the title going away. The championship included a purse of fifty dollars for each racer.

"The guys from Mio were our closest competitors in the Junior Division," Dennis told me recently. "We had to really work hard to beat them, but we did."

Terry and Dennis relaxing after 4th of July race

Dennis and Terry with Michigan Junior Championship trophy

Terry added, "One year the Hillman to Alpena race was held on a very hot day. The Mio guys were close behind us all the way. They actually pulled even with us at one point near Lachine. They were tired too and called over to us to suggest that we agree to cross the finish line together in a tie. Dennis and I wanted nothing to do with that. In fact, it made us mad. We started paddling like heck and left them so far behind that we never saw them again after we rounded the next bend."

"That was one of our best, but hardest races," Dennis smiled as he remembered. "Afterwards we couldn't stop twitching from the cadence of our paddling."

"We had some times," Terry said. "Once we were caught by a big storm at the Walloon Lake race. It was scary. But it's something we did and we'll always take pride in."

Darrell and I did practice for a while, well only for a few days actually. First of all, we weren't strong enough to carry his dad's canoe down to the river on the run - or at all for that matter. Once we got it there we just dragged it up on the bank when we were through. And we weren't tough enough for the grueling routine that canoe racers must bear to prepare to be competitive in the events.

We did get an inkling, however, of just how much training and sacrifice Jack, and the other Kents who raced from time to time, and Merle Klein and the Cross brothers and Dennis and Terry endured to be successful.

As to that race Darrell and I watched from the old willow tree, seems like Terry and Dennis actually edged out the Cross brothers for second. Merle and Jack were first, of course.

THE ATLANTA PLAYERS

By E. Dan Stevens (2008)

The academy awards committee completely ignored us and we all went on to other careers, but for a couple of summers the performing arts were front and center for some of us kids in Atlanta. The years 1952 and 1953, I think, and the big play might have been in 1954. I was nine and ten those summers, or maybe eleven.

Claudia and Bonnie Sherwood initiated and hosted our first venture, a circus in their yard on Pettinger Street. Their family lived on the bottom floor of the old Pettinger house. Stan and Flora lived upstairs.

The house had (and still has) a long porch along the front with steps leading down to the front lawn. The steps served as bleachers for our small (but surely enthusiastic) audience.

That first event had four performers: Claudia, Bonnie, their dog Pepper, and me. Three of us were between eight and ten years old; I don't know about the dog. Mrs. Sherwood helped a lot. She made the costumes, suggested the program, made the fudge and cool-aid we sold, and called her friends to be an audience. I'm not sure if younger brother Craig was old enough to organize the apple-bobbing or fish for prizes games, but someone did.

You may wonder how I got to be the only outsider involved in what was primarily the Sherwood Circus. The answer is simple. The Sherwood sisters were among the many cute girls living in Atlanta in those days, and I liked being where the girls were. I just happened to be visiting them when they decided they needed a ringmaster for their production.

And that's what I was, the ringmaster, top hat and all. Claudia was the dancer, doing numbers and steps taught by her mother (in a very accomplished fashion as I recall). Bonnie was dressed in a clown outfit and also did gymnastic stunts. (She had taken lessons from Mrs. Shirley Peck.) We all did a short skit. Pepper did tricks, mostly sit, stand and stay. His dog hat and tutu outfit more than made up for any staidness in his act.

While Barnum and Bailey didn't exactly beat a path to our door with invitations to join their big show, we did have fun and built some memories that haven't quite left any of us. Sheila Carey mentioned to me at the Fair a few weeks ago that her mother had brought her to the Sherwood Circus. She mostly remembered the dog.

We might have done an encore performance the next summer, none of us can remember, but the Sherwoods moved away sometime about then necessitating a new venue. The obvious choice was my backyard next to the hardware store in the middle of town. We had a ready-made stage, the roof of the old well house originally built by Grove Rouse. It was partially underground in the nature of a root cellar and had housed the equipment to provide potable water and fire protection for the Rouse home and his adjacent hardware business.

The well house still had two wells and the machinery blocks for the pumps when my parents bought the house in 1952. My friends and I used it as our clubhouse/fort, etc. for the next several years. For the play, however, its most important feature was its flat, almost level concrete roof. The roof was three to four feet above ground level and sloped toward the back yard where the audience could sit. It was perfect for a play so long as the performers avoided stepping off the edge.

Since the main cast and protagonists of the circus, the Sherwood sisters and their mother (and, of course, Pepper), had moved away, it was necessary to involve more of the local talent than had participated in the Pettinger Road performances. In fact, most of the kids in and around Atlanta were involved in one capacity or another. Mary Lou Paul, Mary Ann Blamer, Terry Stolicker, Jennie Benson, David Wilson, Harry Dice, Karen Davis, Julie Blamer, my cousins, Edgar, Velda and Sylvia, and Claudia Cameron are a few that come to mind. Zoe and Patsy Brooks sang a duet. I'm sure there were others.

And we had a cause. We planned to donate the proceeds from our ticket sales to the cancer society.

Tickets, yes, we even had printed tickets. Not from the Tribune print shop though; that would have been too costly for our budget in those days. Besides, I had a small printing press I had purchased from an ad on the back cover of a comic book. It wasn't much of a printing press, just large enough to print our tickets, one at a time. It had looked a lot bigger in the comic book picture. (I'd like to say that it was the only time I was misled by a comic book ad, but that wouldn't be true.)

The tickets stated the play's title, place and date, a promise of additional skits and a door prize drawing. It also indicated that the proceeds would go to charity and the price: ten cents.

We worked pretty hard to prepare for the play and to sell tickets. Most of the adults around town bought a ticket; we imagined because they admired our ingenuity, but more likely because they wanted us to stop pestering them and ten cents was cheap at the price for that purpose. Also, they could then tell the next one of us that came into their store that they already had one.

The big day came and went. Not everyone who had purchased tickets attended, but we had an audience of twenty, or so, sitting on chairs we had scrounged and makeshift benches we had constructed with boards on cinder blocks in the backyard. The weather was perfect.

The play and skits came off okay; everyone had a part and most had several. Then came the time for the door prize drawing. Panic! We had forgotten to get a prize.

I consulted with Mary Lou. She went back on the stage and entertained the audience, with what I don't remember, while I ran into my house to find something to serve as the prize. I settled on a North Carolina state flag which I had brought when we moved back to Michigan a few years before. It worked okay. Mrs. Sowers won the drawing and she was from Virginia and went back there every winter.

A few days later, several of us went to the home of the cancer society president and presented her with our play profits, six dollars and ten cents. Not bad at ten cents a ticket. And we had spent some on stuff we needed for the play.

What was the play about? Probably the first thing I ever wrote. I can't remember and neither can anyone else I've talked with. But we all remember Mrs. Sowers winning the flag.

THE ATLANTA FORTY-NINERS

By E. Dan Stevens (2008)

It was 1949 instead of 1849, and it was uranium instead of gold, but Atlanta, Michigan, had its own version of prospecting fever. Although it only lasted a week or so, it involved a pretty significant portion of Atlanta's adult male population in June, 1949.

I think I first heard about it from David Wilson's father, Woodrow, during one of my many dinners at their home while growing up. And my Uncle Grove probably told me about it too; I specifically remember him showing me his old Geiger counter one time. But I had forgotten all about it until seeing a picture of the prospectors at Vernon and Marilyn Klein's house a few weeks ago. Vernon and Jim Smith, two of the few participants still living, filled me in on details of the venture.

Prior to World War II, uranium was far from a household word, but after the war everyone knew about the mineral and how important it was. Stories abounded about uranium discoveries in parts of the United States and Canada and about the instant wealth for those who discovered the valuable ore deposits. Elliot Lake, Ontario, became a boomtown because of uranium discoveries there during the early 50's, becoming the home to twelve mines and a population that went from zero to 25,000 in just five years.

Before the Elliot Lake discoveries, however, there were a number of small finds by prospectors working the Mississagi River area of Ontario. Among those early prospectors were two Atlanta surveyors, Leo Smith and

Grove Stevens. They purchased a Geiger counter in the spring of 1949 and ventured into the Canadian wilderness with a tent, fishing gear and a pretty good sense of direction.

Somewhere northwest of the Trail they began to get positive readings with their counter. Apparently, the readings were over an area too large for them to make claims by themselves, so they called home for help. They got plenty.

"I remember being told that Grove and Leo had called home to say they had found something 'pretty good' and that they needed some guys to 'come up here' to help file mineral claims," Vernon Klein told me. "We came. About thirty-five of us. We had all heard stories about prospectors hitting it big. I guess we all got the fever a little bit.

"Wescott and Bleech, probably the biggest employer in Atlanta, shut down. Most of us working for them headed north. So did our bosses, Gurney Wescott and Veryl Bleech. Just about every able-bodied man in town joined us."

Jim Smith had just returned from his military service that June. "Somebody told me what was going on and the next thing I knew I was in the back of a pickup on my way to Canada," he said. "We stayed in tents and worked hard. Somebody must have fished some because I remember eating trout quite a lot."

Vernon described their work, "We had to survey out forty acres for each claim. We used hand compasses and tape measures. Of course, Grove and Leo were surveyors and more or less supervised. But we had to cut the survey lines by hand, mostly with just axes. No chain saws in those days.

"At each forty acre corner we drove a four-sided stake. Each side faced a parcel for which a claim would be filed and the description and claim information was written on the flat part of the stake. We divided ourselves into small groups to file each claim. I don't know how many claims we actually filed, but there were quite a few. Grove and Leo filed the claim forms with the Canadian government, probably after we left."

"There was some uranium there," Jim Smith reminisced. "But to be marketable it had to test at a certain level. Ours didn't test quite high enough.

"None of us really expected to strike it rich, not that it wouldn't have been nice. It was an adventure, though. I never heard anyone complain about going."

Wow, our own forty-niners. I am amazed every time I look at the picture - four of my uncles, fathers of my classmates and friends from school, town leaders and businessmen from my childhood, my high school principal, and a couple of guys not too much older than me. Just about everyone in town is there except shopkeepers who couldn't close, government officials and the postmaster, although he (Waldo Whitehead) often went with Uncle Grove and the Geiger counter on weekend jaunts to the same area.

A few miles further east and who knows, Elliott Lake might have been called Atlanta Lake.

OF PIRATES, PLAYERS, FIRE AND ICE

By E. Dan Stevens (2008)

As I've been doing these Can't Hardly stories over the past few years I have discovered that my memory was not always complete with regard to some events and participants. Sometimes things had faded from my memory and sometimes there were just parts of the story I simply didn't know.

For example, not long after "Pirates of the Thunder Bay" appeared in the Tribune, Kim Bleech and I had a conversation about the raid on the Briley fort. He was a south-sider, of course, and I had forgotten that he had been in one of the duck boats with Ben Thompson that came ashore behind us as we were defending the fort against a land attack by other south-siders. We north-siders ultimately lost the battle to their two-pronged attack.

Kim also told me where the sticks came from that we all used as swords. "They were survey stakes," he told me. "During the early fifties, there was a big movement by the 'Straight to the Straits' coalition to eliminate the eastward jog of highway M-33 between Mio and Atlanta so that M-33 would truly be the shortest and fastest route from Detroit to the Straits of Mackinac. At one time a new route was surveyed directly south from Atlanta, but the project was abandoned a couple of years later. Those abandoned stakes made perfect swords for both sides during our river war that summer."

And then there was the scolding I got from Mary Ann (Blamer) Marlatt (who has delighted in pointing out my shortcomings since 4th grade) after "The Atlanta Players" appeared. "You forgot one of the main acts in our big production in your back yard. Zoe and Patsy Brooks did a duet."

I had forgotten. Worse was that Patsy?(now Beauregard) was with her when she reminded me. They were both laughing at my attempt to apologize for my omission, or more probably, at the effect the years have had on my memory.

And then Foster Cameron reminded me that I had failed to mention about ice removal from "The Tennis Court" in the Spring so that we could play basketball. During the winter the snow was shoveled off the court so that we could play basketball during recess. Yes, we sometimes played with gloves on.

In the spring the snowbanks around the court would melt some days and the water would flood the court and then freeze at night. Foster lived right across the street and kept an ice spud and coal shovel on his porch. He probably did it more often than any of us, but we all at one time or another borrowed his spud and shovel to chip away the ice so we could play some basketball. Sometimes it wasn't my memory that had lapsed; some events took place before my time. After "The Bobsled" was published, several friends who had grown up here a decade or so before I did told me about the toboggan run that was a feature at the hill east of the Chadwick house during the late 30s and early 40s. It had been built as a WPA project during the depression and was quite an elaborate affair. It had sideboards and was quite a bit longer than the runs we had during the 50s.

A couple of years ago I did a story about Christmas in which I described how warm and comfortable it was to be in the Briley house having a cup of Mrs. (Marion) Briley's hot chocolate on Christmas morning. I failed to mention that their house was heated by a coal furnace. It was one of the last homes in Atlanta to use coal, although the school building was coal-heated until at least the late fifties. Art Ferguson delivered the coal.

The Briley basement furnace had an automatic stoker and used a grade of coal that had been crushed to gravel-sized pieces. Once or twice a day, depending on the weather, Darrell or Dennis or Mr. Briley had to fill the stoker, a large rectangular bin in front of the furnace which was connected to the fire box by an auger-like device. Of course, Darrell's friends got to help when we were in a hurry to go ice skating or sledding on a Saturday morning. We had to fill the stoker by shovel from the coal room before he could leave.

Several other of my friends' homes were heated with basement wood furnaces. These furnaces were not at all like the air-tight wood space heaters or stand-alone wood furnaces in use today. They were large fire boxes housed within a galvanized metal heat collection and duct system that resembled a giant octopus. Ducts sprouted from the main furnace enclosure upwards to floor vents in each room above. The warm air generated by the burning wood rose naturally through the ducts to heat the house.

I helped get in the wood for the winter at least a couple of times at my friend David Wilson's house. Over the course of the summer David's father, Woodrow, had cut and hauled several loads of small tree trunks from the woods to a stack behind their house. He hauled the wood on a two-wheel trailer pulled by a John Deere B tractor.

Then, usually in early September, on a Saturday when David and one or two of his friends were out of school, we would "buzz" the wood. The buzz saw was attached to the front of the John Deere. It had an axle with a saw on one end and a flat pulley on the other. It also had a hinged tray on which the logs were placed and pushed into the saw and cut into stove-length pieces. The saw was powered by a belt from the tractor's pulley.

Woodrow and a helper worked the buzz saw; David and I picked up the sawed firewood pieces and threw them into the basement through the open outside door. After we finished at his house, we crossed the road and did the same at his grandmother's (Mrs. Harper's) house. It was a long day by the time both woodpiles had been cut and thrown into the basements.

Although I never had to go with them (after all, there were six Marlatt boys) I remember Saturdays when Tuffy and Punky weren't available for whatever we had planned because they had to help Uncle Buster buzz their winter wood.

Note: *Where appropriate, I have incorporated some of these later-learned items in the stories as I edited for this book. EDS*

THE LUMBERJACK PATROL

By E. Dan Stevens (2009)

Dick Kimberly and Jerry Diehl were short-time residents of Atlanta, only for a year or two during 1954 and 1955. They and their wives were the proprietors of the Atlanta Sports Shop, having purchased it from and then sold it back to Glen and Jean Erity. But during their brief tenure, they started Troop 89, Atlanta, Michigan, Boy Scouts of America. I think Dick had previous experience with the Scouts in southern Michigan.

After Dick and Jerry moved back down-state, Jack McMurphy and probably one or two others kept it going, and then Leon Genre and Bill Boden, who together operated the cabinet shop for Doty Lumber Company, took over leadership of Troop 89 and continued in that capacity all the while I was a member of the troop. A number of other men in Atlanta, some fathers of scouts, others not, helped Leon and Bill with troop activities. Later Colen Wilson started and led an Explorer Scout group when some of us became too old for the regular Boy Scouts.

This story is about our boy scouting days. I don't think Troop 89 was all that typical of scouting in general; for example, none of us were that gung-ho about merit badges or promotions in class, and quite a few of us never did end up with a complete uniform, although most of us had the regulation shirt. We did participate in some regional scouting activities and for several summers some of us attended Boy Scout Camp Greilick over near Traverse City.

One of our first undertakings was to organize our troop into patrols, six or so scouts in each. I'm not sure how we were divided, but the troop ended up with at least four patrols. Nearly every boy between twelve and fourteen from town and the surrounding area was a member.

My patrol was a little different from the start. While the other patrols chose a name listed in the scout manual, such as the Wolf Patrol or Fox Patrol or the like, we decided to be original; we called ourselves the Lumberjack Patrol.

We were pretty proud of ourselves for choosing a name that was not only unique in scouting, but was somewhat indigenous to our locale. However, there was a price for being different. The other patrols could order their flags and patches from the scout catalog; we had to design and make our own.

One of our number drew an axe and cross-cut saw crossed in the middle. Fortunately, another of our members was Johnny Plumley whose mother, Anna, could make anything imaginable from cloth. Soon we had a flag, black on red, and patches that were the envy of all the other patrols.

I can only remember one Lumberjack Patrol activity independent from the rest of the troop. We stayed at my dad's cabin on Camp 8 Road for the opening weekend of trout season one year, accompanied by Mr. McMurphy. One of our parents helped with transportation on Friday after school, along with some grub and supplies, and came back Sunday to pick us up. I think we were a little light on the food, fully expecting to supplement it with fresh trout. We were within walking distance of Gingell Lake and several spots along Gingell Creek as it got larger near the East Branch of the Black River.

It was too cold to fish comfortably, but we did it anyway. Most of us gave up sometime Saturday morning after catching none or only a few undersized trout. We had taken sandwiches with us for lunch while fishing, but most of us had returned to the cabin before noon and ate our sandwiches around the warm wood stove.

Two didn't make it back for lunch, Bobby Brooks and Austin Briley. They had headed the furthest downstream on Gingell Creek, walking nearly a mile north of the cabin on Camp 8 Road and then following an old logging trail east to the stream.

It was nearly dark when they finally returned to the cabin. Their bags were loaded with brook trout, though it was clear they hadn't used a ruler when keeping many of them. The rest of us quickly abandoned our plans for a pancake dinner and began melting butter in the big frying pan. A good meal was had by all.

On the other hand, Troop 89 had many activities that included all of us. Leon and Bill must have liked cold weather camping because we had at least three challenging camping trips during those years. The first was at the old CCC camp at Clear Lake in the fall and involved several other troops from our region. I think our meals were prepared in the old camp dining hall, but we slept outside in tents. It was raining nearly the whole time, cold, and hard to get out of the sleeping bag in the morning. Most of us slept with our clothes on so we only had to put on shoes in order to scurry to breakfast.

Our next two were winter ventures were at the Atlanta Rod and Gun Club. On one of those trips we cooked our own meals outside on campfires. Someone had brought some frozen fish sticks, fortunately a lot of them, which turned out to be quite popular cooked in an open frying pan. As I recall, the nighttime temperature reached negative numbers both nights we were there that year.

The next time we went, Bill Huey came along and cooked for us in the club's kitchen. Most of us still slept outside in tents. A couple of the guys were allowed to sleep inside for medical reasons, and of course, so did the adults.

During our second night the sleeping bags and cold ground outside became more unpleasant to endure, so several of us sneaked into the lodge and went upstairs to sleep on the floor next to our lucky friends. We were quiet but didn't sleep much. Just before dawn we crept down the stairs and went back out to our tents.

During all this time, our scoutmaster, Leon Genre, was asleep on a bunk at the bottom of the stairs. We knew he was asleep because he never stopped snoring. The thing is, Leon had been severely wounded in World War II. One of his eyes was unable to close. At breakfast he named each one of us who had gone in and out during the night, claiming to have seen us with his eye that never closed. We were shocked at his accuracy. I spent quite a bit of time with Leon after that over a number of years and never discovered whether he had actually seen us while fast asleep or learned our names from another source.

I came upon an old Tribune article recently about a contribution from the Atlanta Lions Club to help us attend Camp Greilick one year. The attendees were Jim Basch, Rod Marlatt, Bob Teets, Robin McMurphy, Joe Chadwick, Ollin Hiller, Larry Wilson and me. Bud Teets and my dad drove us over.

TROUT FISHING WITH TUFFY - PART III

By E. Dan Stevens (2009)

"D____, these mosquitoes are thick and they're biting," I said to Tuffy as I slapped one on my wrist, splattering blood that the vicious little insect had already extracted. We were standing next to an old beaver dam, preparing our rods to go after the brook trout we fully expected to be in this part of our favorite fishing river. It was early June, our first trip here of the year. School had ended the Friday before.

"The trout don't start biting until the mosquitoes do," he responded, a saying I'd heard from him before, "so get out the six-twelve and we'll go fishing." Six-twelve was the most popular mosquito repellent in those days, effective, but at a price; it had a terrible smell. Your girl-friend wouldn't be inclined to cozy up much after you had spread it over your exposed skin areas.

I reached into the front pocket of my fishing bag and was aware immediately that something was wrong, it was wet and a little sticky. Then I felt the broken glass. The six-twelve bottle had broken, probably as I had struggled to hang on to the John Deere B fender which had been my seat during our ride from the Marlatt farm to the river.

It was Uncle Buster's tractor and we didn't exactly have his permission to take it that day, but we planned to have it back before he returned from work. He was the mechanic at the Atlanta Hardware, then a John Deer tractor and implement dealer.

"The bottle broke," I exclaimed. "The dope all leaked out. We're gonna get eaten alive."

Tuffy turned back toward the tractor. "I've got something else," he said. "We didn't come way out here for nothing."

It was our first trip to our favorite stream for native trout, but not our first time trout fishing that year. We had both joined a hoard of others on the Thunder Bay River below the Atlanta Dam on opening day and a couple of the Saturdays during May. And I had fished Canada Creek with Jim Durkee a couple of times as well. But those fish were mostly hatchery raised, browns and rainbows planted in the Thunder Bay, brookies in Canada Creek.

Trout fishing was a much bigger deal in those days. The motels and cabins and even the old Atlanta Hotel were fully booked weeks before for the last weekend in April. That Saturday was always opening day. Until the Department of Conservation redirected its resources to make the Great Lakes a salmon fishery, its primary focus during the mid-sixties, its hatchery program had been mostly directed at the state's more traditional stream and inland lake sport fisheries.

But fishing the unplanted streams had been special for Tuffy and me ever since he first took me to Barger Creek when I was nine. The native brookies seemed to bite better a little later in the year, or as Tuffy said, when the mosquitoes really got going.

Tuffy was Lawrence Marlatt, but only his mother called him Lawrence. As he got older some people called him Larry, but to most of us he was always Tuffy. It was the same with his brothers Donald, Raymond and Rodney. Don, the oldest, was Sonny, and still is to most of us. Ray was Butch and Rod was Punky. Only Ron and Harvey of the six Marlatt brothers were known by their given names during their school years.

But I digress; Tuffy returned from the tractor with a pack of Crooks cigars, crooked and rum soaked.

"These will work," he said, offering one to me. "Just puff on it. The smoke will keep the mosquitoes away."

If he told me where he got them, it has long slipped my mind. He was fourteen that summer; I was twelve. I doubt that he could have bought them directly from a store. At any rate it was my first cigar.

Did it keep the mosquitoes at bay? I don't remember. It must have to some extent because I don't recall getting eaten alive as we might have been with no mosquito protection at all. What I do remember is that the cigar made me sick as a dog. We caught a few trout at first, but it wasn't long before I was lying on the riverbank, too queasy to even cast my line in the water.

When we finally decided to leave, I couldn't even take my turn on the flywheel that had to be spun to start the Model B. The tractor ride back wasn't too cool either. Tuffy had to stop for my nausea a couple of times.

And worse, when we got back Uncle Buster was waiting for us. He had come home for lunch and found his tractor gone. He must have guessed where it was because our promise not to take it again without his permission along with our offer to share the trout with him seemed to resolve the issue.

Tuffy and I visited our favorite spot quite a few times after that, but never again by tractor. His "mosquito dope" of choice changed to Philly Cheroots and later in life, even when not fishing, he usually had a pack of them in his shirt pocket. I would occasionally puff on one while at the river with him, but mostly I was very careful not to break the six-twelve bottle again.

A SCHOOL BUS ON SLEIGHS

as told by Maurice Carey (2009)

He was born in 1921, the year after his father, a veterinarian, and mother moved to their newly purchased farm just west of Atlanta, Michigan. (He and his twin brother were between an older brother and sister and a younger brother and sister.) Since then Maurice Carey has been a long-time Briley Township Supervisor, a member of the Montmorency County Board of Supervisors (now Board of County Commissioners), and worked at various jobs in and around Atlanta, including being active in a number of volunteer activities, not the least of which has been the Montmorency County 4-H Fair.

But he never left that land. Maurice and his late wife Onalee (whom he met roller skating at the old Atlanta School Community Building) bought the farm from his parents and the Carey legacy has continued with their children growing up there as well. Maurice still lives in the old family house.

"My first school was the McKenzie School, the one that has been moved to the fairgrounds", Maurice Carey reminisced recently. "I walked about a mile each way. Before school was over we moved back downstate, and I finished my first year there. When we moved back the next summer, 1927, the McKenzie School had been closed, soon to be purchased by the Michigan Grange, so we had to go to the Atlanta school.

"The school board didn't have any regular school buses for its new students, instead opting to contract with Harrison Baker to transport the country students to town for school. Harrison purchased a Ford truck chassis and hired Mac McTaggert, a local blacksmith, to build a shed-like body on the back to shelter the students on the way to and from school.

"It was more like a shack than a bus body. Mac used regular house windows, for example. I remember that the state bus inspector complained several times the bus body didn't meet regulations because there was no way to open those windows, but no changes were ever made. Also, it had truck suspension and was very rough riding for us students. The tires weren't very good in snow either.

"In fact, we had too much snow that year, 1927, for the truck to travel the back roads safely. Harrison's solution was to engage Mr. McTaggert to build a shed on a set of sleighs. It was actually a big improvement. We had a brooder stove for heat. The wood fire made it quite cozy and the smooth ride of the horse drawn sleighs was a vast improvement over the truck.

"Eventually the snow melted and we had to go back to the truck to everyone's chagrin. Fortunately, in a few years the school board contracted for a regular school bus. It was a vast improvement over the truck, but most of us probably would have chosen the sleighs again if we had had the chance."

Twenty years later Maurice himself began a ten year stint as a school bus driver for the Atlanta School. The buses then were pretty much the same as school buses today but had a red, white and blue color scheme.

"I guess better snow plowing eliminated the need for sleighs," Maurice said, chuckling. "But everything was harder in those days. Our father was very strict, made us work long, hard hours on the farm.

"One time my twin brother, Mercer, had saved enough money to buy an old Ford Model T pickup that was for sale, but Dad wouldn't let him. He reasoned that having the pickup would enable Mercer to get away from his farm chores. I think for the same reason he never let us have bikes when we were growing up.

"Of course, we didn't do just farm work. Sometimes one or the other of us would go with Dad on veterinary calls. I remember a call for two cows that the Remingtons, then owners of the Big Rock Store, had fed some unripe field beans. The cows were bloating something awful until Dad surgically removed the beans. The cows survived.

"A man named Ross Becker often landed his old biplane in a field just east of our farm," Maurice continued. "Mr. Becker was pretty well known for his stunt flying. One time on the Fourth of July during a base-ball game he did a spiral dive down toward the ball field, then located on M-32 across from the Full Gospel Church. It scared everyone but he managed to pull up in what seemed the nick of time.

"One time when Mr. Becker had landed at our neighbor's farm, Dad offered to take us boys over to see the airplane. There was a catch, though: we had to hoe a cornfield first after supper. We set out hoeing, but Gates who was the most excited about seeing the plane hurried through his rows with some obvious results: he missed a lot of the weeds. When Dad saw the outcome he made us do all of Gates' rows again before he took us over to see the old biplane - not so old then, I guess.

"I remember that Dad told us to look with our eyes, not our hands. Made it hard for us to climb into the cockpit. At any rate, my brother Gates was smitten. When he and Eldon Dobbyn enlisted during World War II they went to the same base for training. Gates took an exam for flying and passed. Eldon always said that Gates was the only one on the whole base who did. He ended up becoming a B-17 pilot and flew thirty bombing missions from a base in Great Britain. He stayed in the Air Force through the Vietnam War."

When Mercer also enlisted and his parents moved to Bay City, Maurice was left to operate the farm. He did that and much more over the next fifty-five years. And incidentally, the part about better snow plowing making the school bus sleighs obsolete, well, Maurice did some of that too during the eight years he worked for the Montmorency County Road Commission.

THE HIRED HANDS

By E. Dan Stevens (2009)

"Hey," Claudia said to me at a multi-class Atlanta High School reunion earlier this summer at the Clear Lake State Park, "look around. Except for Darrell, the whole Can't Hardly crew is here."

Sure enough, I looked over and saw Bob Teets talking to Larry Wilson under a nearby pine tree. They and I, together with Darrell Briley, had been the partners, owners, proprietors, woodcutters, haulers, stackers and almost everything else for the Can't Hardly Lumber Company which harvested pulpwood on my dad's farm during the summer of 1960. But we didn't do quite everything; we had three hired hands for a short while. As I looked around I saw that all of them were at the reunion, too.

It all started after our first load of poplar pulpwood was sold to the Abitibi paper mill in Alpena. The trucker who picked it up, Chaney Fox I think, told us that we could get an extra fourteen dollars a cord for the wood if it was peeled. He also pointed out that it was pretty easy to peel poplar that time of year with the use of peeling tools if done immediately after a tree was felled.

That got us to thinking, of course. An extra fourteen dollars per cord would be almost a fifty percent increase in our revenue. So that night I rounded up a couple of peeling tools, made from half of a car spring leaf welded to a short length of pipe. The pipe was used as the handle and the other end of the spring was ground down to a flat, almost sharp edge.

The next day we tried out the new tools. After a tree was cut and the limbs removed, we ran the chain saw along the vertical length of the tree, cutting just deep enough to get through the bark. Then two of us inserted tools under the bark along the cut line. Because of the sap between the bark and the wood, the bark slid away from the trunk over the entire tree length quite easily in most cases. One exception was where large limbs had grown. Also, a few trees had less sap or thinner bark, either of which condition would decrease the effectiveness of the peeling tools.

After peeling, we cut the trunks into eight-foot lengths and hauled them to a new section of our woodpile. At the end of the day we tallied our results. We had actually come out behind. The time spent peeling had been taken from our normal cutting and hauling time, and even with the increased value of the peeled wood our volume had decreased to the point that our total earnings were less.

We were riding home in my '37 Chevrolet when Darrell Briley said out of the blue, "We should hire some people to peel the trees and we should concentrate on our cutting and hauling."

"Good idea," Larry agreed, "but who?"

"I think I know who," Darrell responded. When he told us, we all agreed.

So that night we met at Steve's Place with our prospective employees, Mary Ann Blamer, Claudia Cameron and Judy Brown.

"Sounds like fun," Claudia volunteered.

"Going to the woods with you guys? I don't know," Mary Ann mused.

"Sounds like work," Judy concluded, demonstrating clearly that she best grasped the concept of our proposal.

But we persisted. Soon all three agreed that we would pick them up bright and early the next morning for their first day of pulpwood peeling.

So we did. It meant taking two cars. Larry and Bob and Mary Ann and Judy rode in my '37 Chevy; Claudia rode on the beach chair which served as the second seat in Darrell's homemade sports car.

The day started out in a promising fashion. The first tree peeled quite easily, but the second was another matter. It had thin bark and didn't seem to have much sap either. That might have been the first time I heard girls use certain words which I cannot repeat here. Darrell and I helped out with that tree and several more as the morning wore on. We also noticed Bob and Larry spending quite a bit of time where the girls were. In retrospect, I guess it was more fun to help the girls than to do our regular jobs.

By noon it was clear that it wasn't going to work. All three girls were dragging. After all, pretty girls weren't expected to be in the kind of shape necessary to work in the woods. Also, Mary Ann had been right; having the girls there in the woods with us was mighty distracting. We cut and hauled less than half as much as we normally did.

Over our lunches we made an executive decision: we would take the girls back to town - and everyone would go to Clear Lake for a swim. Sort of a retirement party for the girls, you see. No wood was cut that afternoon.

The next morning Larry, Bob, Darrell and I were back at it, *sans* the peeling tools and our hired hands.

So, we had a little Can't Hardly reunion at the school reunion. Claudia went over to get Mary Ann and Judy, and I went over to snag Larry and Bob. While waiting, we noticed the three ladies having a discussion and laughing as they walked toward us.

When they arrived, Mary Ann said, "We were trying to figure out how much a half-day's minimum wage for the three of us would be after forty-nine years of adding and compounding interest. You guys never did pay us, you know."

TANK'S TOUCHDOWN

By E. Dan Stevens (2009)

I had just carried out my fake to the right side and was looking back to watch Tank Wilson who had gotten the ball over the middle in our effort to pick up a first down from our own forty-eight yard line. The first down marker was just past the fifty. I glanced up in time to see the Hale safety bounce off and sprawl on the ground as Tank broke into the clear. Their middle linebacker was already flat on his back and no other defenseman was within ten yards as Tank rumbled toward the end zone.

It was only the fifth year that Atlanta had fielded a high school football team, but already there was a tradition of long touchdown runs by Atlanta fullbacks. Tom May ran ninety-eight yards from scrimmage to pay dirt during the first year, and Ray Marlatt and Kim Bleech had a number of long scoring runs the next year, although some were probably from the halfback position. Tuffy Marlatt and Brian Moline, respectively, continued the tradition of long dashes as the team's fullbacks over the ensuing two years.

Finally, in our senior year, Tank was moved from right tackle to the fullback position. We had a pretty good team that year, winning close games at Onaway and Hillman to claim Atlanta's first North Star League football championship. Of course, in those days the Lewiston school district students attended high school in Atlanta and made up a significant part of our team. In addition to Tom May and Brian Moline, Ed Schroeder and many others had been leaders on the AHS team in prior years and four of my six fellow seniors on the team had attended the Lewiston school before their high school days in Atlanta. Dick Scarsella had attended the Loud school also, but Ed Boettcher, Bob Korph and Doug Mowery had been in Lewiston for their elementary and junior high school years. Only Tank, Jimmy Utt and I attended Atlanta before high school. (David Wilson, also a senior, would have been on the team had he not been injured.)

We had taken our knocks during our previous football seasons, especially during our sophomore year after the really good athletes of the class of '58 had graduated, but here we were playing Hale in our third from the last game of the season. With three more wins we would be our school's first football league champs. We had experience and we had good coaching. Lyle "Red" McDonnell had been the head coach for all five years of the program and George Pinchock, Al Hamilton and Tuffy were assistants. George and Al had been football stars at Beecher High School in Flint.

And we had good underclassmen. Juniors Robin McMurphy, Jim Basch, Joe Swartz, Austin Briley, Bob Teets, Fred Heine, Charlie Johnson, Phil Korph and Joel Secrist were really the team's stalwarts. Sophomore Butch Georgi and Freshman Lyle Klein were also starters and several of their classmates contributed a lot to the team.

But I digress. Tank was our leader, our captain and the team's MVP that year. His nickname was indicative of not only his physical stature, but also of his tenacity and ability to play football. As a tackle he could block with the best of them. As our middle linebacker, he made more tackles than most of the rest of us put together. And he was a devastating blocker from the fullback position on sweeps and reverses.

However, he had never made a long run for a touchdown. He was unstoppable in short yardage situations and accounted for many of our first downs. It usually took two or three defenders to stop his forward momentum when the Tank got going, but usually the needed additional tacklers would catch up with him as he dragged the first one along.

So I watched with amazement as he broke into the clear and galloped toward the east end zone of Doty Field. He crossed the forty yard line, then the thirty-five. Still no opponent was within ten yards as he steamed along. Neither were any of his teammates close enough to block for him, but it didn't look like he would need any blocks to reach pay dirt. He crossed the thirty and the twenty-five, and then the twenty. He was going to make it!

When he was at about the fifteen yard line, I could see him reach down toward his belt. Then his pants started falling down with each stride he took. He tried to pull them up, but they were down far enough to restrain his leg movements. He struggled on while trying to pull his football pants high enough to run again. He crossed the ten with the nearest defender closing in.

Suddenly the pants fell down to his knees and he started to trip. The Hale defender arrived at the same time and they tumbled to the ground together at the five yard line. Tank's dash was over. His long touchdown run was not to be.

He managed to get his pants back up and was able to hold them as he trotted stiffly off the field. The rest of us tried not to laugh as he went by the huddle. When he got to the sideline, the coaches tried desperately to fix his belt, but it had completely broken in two.

I think someone in the stands loaned him a belt so he could get back in the game, but alas, he was too late. Joe Swartz ran around end for the touchdown on the next play. Tank was still getting his belt fixed.

Recently I had the opportunity of telling this story to Tank's son. He liked the story but was puzzled when I kept referring to his dad as Tank. During our school years and for a few years after we all had called him that, but for the past thirty years or so we had gone back to calling him by his real name, Larry.

THE KLONDIKE DERBY

By E. Dan Stevens (2010)

We were losing. I don't remember how many teams we were up against, but there were at least two from Alpena and others from Rogers City, Hillman, Onaway and Posen. There might have been more. It was the Klondike Derby, a Boy Scout event held each winter at the Hoeft State Park near Rogers City. Our Atlanta troop was participating that year for the first time.

We weren't running last, but we were close. It was a dog sled race; we were the dogs. In the weeks before the event each troop had constructed a sled along the lines of a dog sled to be used in the competition. The course was a series of several stations, each with an associated task to be accomplished by the participants before departing for the next. I remember that the requirements for one of the stations was to build a fire using wood collected and cut at a previous station and bring a pot of water to a boil. The water was derived from melting snow.

Hoeft State Park is situated on the shore of Lake Huron a few miles northwest of Rogers City. Its southerly boundary is the US-23 highway. Cedar swamps, pine knolls, marshes and, of course, a big sandy beach make up its landscape. I vividly remember the large ice structures created along the beach and for several yards offshore by the pounding waves. It was the first time I had ever been on a Great Lake shoreline in the winter.

The conversation must have gone something like this:

"We need more wood. This water will never boil."

"Only the wood we collected at the last station can be used according to the rules."

"Can we burn part of the sled?"

Our inexperience was showing. Most of the other troops had previous Klondike Derby experience, but this was our first one.

Not that we hadn't had previous winter outings. Our scoutmasters, Leon Genre and Bill Boden, had taken us on at least two winter camping trips to the Atlanta Rod and Gun Club property north of town. We had slept in tents and cooked some of our meals over campfires in the subfreezing weather, but the club's heated lodge was available for some of our meals and other uses.

Just as we were thinking that we would have to backtrack to the previous station, the water started to boil. But one more team had passed us while we were waiting.

Each team had six participants. Ours were Larry Wilson, Robin McMurphy, Bob Teets and me, and I think, Austin Briley and Harry Dice. As I said, this was our first time. We didn't know what to expect, but it turned out to be a very enjoyable day for all of us.

While we had been waiting for the water to boil, we had been taking turns rereading the derby rules and examining the park map. More discussion:

"The rules don't require us to do each station in order."

"And we don't have to follow the trails."

"What if we cut across the marsh over there and do the last two stations next, and then we could backtrack along the trail for six and five. See, station five is very close to the finish if we go cross-country."

"I don't know..."

"If it's a better way, why aren't the other teams doing it?"

"Maybe they haven't figured it out."

"What if the marsh isn't frozen?"

"We'll probably fall in. I don't want to get wet. There's no place to dry out."

"One of us could go ahead with a pole to check the ice."

"What have we got to lose? We aren't going to catch the teams ahead of us if we stay on the trail."

"Why not?"

"Okay."

"We didn't come here to be last."

Everyone nodded. So when the water started to boil, we were off. At first it didn't look very promising. There was a huge snow drift at the edge of the marsh and it took all of us pushing and pulling to get the sled through. But once we were past the drift we found that the winds had blown the marsh ice nearly clear of snow. It only took us a few minutes to reach the trail on the other side.

None of the other teams had reached either of the last two stations. We did the tasks at the last one first and then the next to last one. We headed back up the trail toward station six. Along the way we met one of the Alpena teams which was way ahead of everyone else.

They seemed to think we were lost. We might have encouraged them to think that. We asked them where station six was. They laughed at us while pointing behind them.

We arrived at station six a few seconds before the team running second along the regular trail. It was a good thing because only one team could do the station six task at a time. They had to wait for us to finish instead of vice versa.

By the time we reached station five we had met most of the other teams. They all thought we were lost and going the wrong way. We could hear their snickers.

The task at station five was a simple one and was quickly accomplished. According to the map the finish line was only a few hundred yards north. We looked in that direction. It was a steep hill covered with white pine trees

I think our resolve suffered a little, but we had no choice. We headed up that hill pushing and pulling our sled. Luck was with us. The snow under the pines was only a few inches deep and we were soon at the top.

The finish was right ahead down the slope. Several officials were milling about and looking back up the trail. The Alpena team was about the same distance as us from the finish, actually a gate of sorts. Nobody had seen us yet and the Alpena guys were goofing off a little, jumping on and off their sled to see who could ride across the finish.

We started running down the hill, pulling our sled. About halfway down we started yelling. The Alpena guys finally saw us and started running too, but not in time. Our sled passed through the gate a good ten yards ahead of theirs.

They didn't declare us the winners right away, but after a meeting among Leon Genre, the Alpena scoutmaster and the officials, everyone agreed that we had won fair and square.

Afterwards we sat at the head table for the awards picnic in the pavilion, hot dogs and sausages. Did I mention that some of the best kielbasa and brats in the world are made right there in Rogers City?

CONTRABAND

By E. Dan Stevens (2010)

The two-tone green Nash Rambler cruised slowly down the main drag toward us, heading west. We were sitting on the tongue of a new John Deere hay bailer next to the Atlanta Hardware. The new bailer was on a vacant lot between the hardware store and the bank. A few years later Jack Paul would build his insurance office on the lot, but in the early 50's Carl Briley used it to display John Deere tractors and implements as part of his hardware business.

All of us recognized the car; it belonged to Deputy Sheriff Sam Moss, one of three deputies to Montmorency County Sheriff Charles Brown. The other two were Joel Secrist, who lived and worked mostly in Lewiston, and Doc Eagle, who lived and worked mostly in Hillman. They, along with Stella Brown who ran the jail located in the basement of the old Courthouse, were the totality of Montmorency County law enforcement then, except in those rare instances when the State Police was called in. All four, the deputies and Sheriff Brown, used their personal automobiles to carry out their law enforcement duties.

None of us gave much thought to Deputy Moss until he suddenly swerved and stopped along the curb directly in front of us. It was a hot day, at least by northern Michigan standards, the 6th or 7th of July, so all of the Rambler's windows were rolled down. No air-conditioning in those days.

Deputy Moss leaned across the front seat, pointed at me and barked, "Stevens, get in."

I sat stunned for a few seconds, wondering what I might have done. He repeated himself in an even harsher tone and pushed the passenger door open toward me. Still puzzled, I did as he said.

"Shut the door," he commanded, and when I did so he pulled away from the curb and headed out of town, still going west.

It then dawned on me; this was the aftermath of a little run in Austin Briley and I had experienced with Sheriff Brown and Deputy Moss in the small parking area between Doty Lumber Company and Mason and Mills Gulf Station a few days earlier on the 4th of July.

Atlanta celebrated the 4th of July in grand style in those days. Activities took place over several days. They included a breakfast and bingo tent located on the Forrester's Ford Garage used car lot, open for the entire celebration; a canoe race which started and ended at the dam, with to and from and several laps around Lake 15 in between; a baseball game at Doty Field; races and other events for children each day of the celebration; and the parade and fireworks over the river on the 4th. The length of the festivities might vary depending on which day of the week the 4th fell on, but the parade and fireworks were always on the 4th itself.

It was an exciting time for us kids. There was no age limit to play bingo; all you needed was a nickel. And a little patience since the benches and tables surrounding the bingo caller were often shoulder to shoulder with players. One year a B-B gun was a prize choice. Needless to say, it was the goal of every boy who didn't already have one to win it. I blame Dick May for my failure in that regard.

Dick May was the hawker for all things relating to the Atlanta 4th of July celebration. During the entire two or three days of activities he drove around town with two large megaphone shaped speakers on top of his car announcing which events were ongoing or about to begin. His car must have had an automatic transmission (not too common in those days) because I still picture him driving slowly around town with one hand on the steering wheel and the other holding a big square silver-colored microphone in front of his mouth as he gave his spiel.

Well, I was about to sit down at the bingo tent with a dime (thanks mom) to buy two cards when I heard, "The three-legged race will start in ten minutes." Mr. May was announcing from his car parked by the tent.

No way could I be sure the next bingo game would be finished in time and I had promised to partner with David Wilson for the race. Since the B-B gun had not been claimed for nearly a day already and all of the players at the table looked too old to want it, I felt confident it would still be there after the race. So off to the park I ran.

Too bad the phrase "good news, bad news" hadn't been coined then because it would have applied to my decision to abandon my place at the bingo table to participate in the three legged race. It was good that David and I won the race and each received a silver dollar for our effort. I was already calculating the number of cards I could get with my new-found wealth as I ran back to the bingo tent. But it was not so good to see a grown man walking away with the B-B gun when I got there. I guess he must have had a son who wanted one too.

But I wasn't thinking about bingo as Deputy Moss drove west on M-32. I was thinking about walking with Austin Briley past the Doty Lumber Company store after the parade a few days earlier and tossing a lit firecracker into the street just as I realized that Sheriff Brown and Deputy Moss were standing in the driveway between Doty's and the Mason and Mills Gulf Station.

We couldn't hide what we were doing; the officers were only about twenty feet away from us. Of course almost all fireworks were illegal then, including the small firecrackers we had.

"Hand 'em over boys," Sheriff Brown ordered as he held out his hand.

We obeyed. That was that, I thought, until now. Was Deputy Moss going to tell my parents? They would definitely not be pleased with me. Maybe he was going to give me a chance to tell them first. Wouldn't make much difference.

He pulled over on the shoulder and stopped. We were across from the Full Gospel Church. He reached under his seat and pulled out a bag. "Take these out to your farm," he said as he handed me the bag full of the firecrackers they had taken from Austin and me on the 4th. "Just don't use them around town anymore."

I can't remember what I did do with those firecrackers, but I'm pretty sure I didn't take them out to the farm. It would have been pretty boring to make noise when no one can hear.

CUTTING CHRISTMAS TREES

By E. Dan Stevens (2011)

"Yikes!" I heard Bob yell, followed by equally loud shouts of pain, anger and frustration. I dropped my bushman saw and ran as fast as I could toward where I had last seen him, though the going was tough through the clumps of dried weeds and the balsam and spruce trees in the featherbed marsh where we were working. It was the Saturday following Thanksgiving in 1955 or 1956. Bob Teets and I were cutting Christmas trees on my dad's farm in Pleasant Valley.

Bob had stopped yelling by the time I got to him and was looking down at his bloodied boot. I could see the sharp, double-bitted axe he had been using to fell a balsam fir implanted in its stump.

Back then Christmas tree farms were not common, if they existed at all, in northern Michigan. Christmas trees were harvested from the wild. They were mostly balsam fir and white spruce, both of which were, and still are, plentiful in the swamps and marshes throughout Montmorency and its surrounding counties.

For many woodcutters and farmers, late November and early December provided a short-lived opportunity for extra income from cutting Christmas trees. My uncle, Olin Stevens, Jim Kent and several others went at it in a big way. I remember each year seeing huge piles of trees in Olin's front yard across from the Gulf Station in Atlanta and at Jim's house on M-32 West awaiting trucks which would haul them to Christmas tree sale lots in Flint and Detroit. I also recall similar stacks of trees on the Beaman Smith farm east of town and at other farms as well.

Many of the Christmas tree cutters sold their trees to southern Michigan retailers, but a few would rent a vacant lot someplace downstate from which they would retail the trees they had harvested and purchased from other local cutters. This was often a route to much greater profits from their trees.

My dad, too, and his lumberjacks usually cut Christmas trees from his farm and other lands that he might be timbering. For several years I was able to make a few dollars by cutting trees at the farm which would then be sold by Dad. Often one or more of my friends would help and share in the proceeds, a dollar or two a tree, as I recall.

It was not as easy as it sounds. Unlike the modern tree farm where trees are harvested when they reach ideal Christmas tree heights of five to eight feet, most of the trees we cut were the tops of much larger trees, often fifty feet in height. Using only an axe and bushman saw, we would fell the larger tree and then cut off the top part to be the actual Christmas tree. (The following spring my dad's crew would come along and cut up the rest of the tree for pulpwood.)

One year, though, Dad decided to venture downstate to sell his trees. I believe it was 1958. A friend of his from there arranged for a vacant lot to be rented in what is now the city of Westland. Dad's crew loaded his freshly cut trees on his logging truck, a 1957 Chevrolet, and he and one of his crew, Roy Gammey, set out for the rented lot.

They arrived on December 10th and unloaded and arranged the trees around the lot and put up a hand-painted sign to advertise that Christmas trees were for sale. My brother Bob, then a student in Ann Arbor, joined Dad and Roy at the tree lot on weekends, and then full time when his Christmas vacation began. Mother brought me down to help for the last week before Christmas. I stayed with Dad's friend who lived nearby, but Dad, Bob and Roy slept in a rented house trailer on the lot.

Most of the trees were priced from five to ten dollars, but we had one nine feet tall, a perfectly shaped spruce tree that Dad had priced at twenty dollars. On the weekend before Christmas we were very busy, all four of us constantly taking money and loading and tying trees on top of cars. Dad finally took fifteen dollars for the perfect spruce and by mid-afternoon on Christmas Eve we were down to ten or so scraggly trees. We decided to close up and go home.

After discarding most of the unsold trees at a nearby landfill, and since only three of us could ride in the cab, we made a cushy bed on the truck bed just behind the cab with boughs from the remaining trees. Roy got into his sleeping bag on the boughs and we covered him and some presents we had purchased with a canvas. By the time we stopped in Flint for gas it had started to rain. Bob offered to change places with Roy, but Roy seemed satisfied with his arrangement.

The rain had turned to snow somewhere north of Bay City, and we had to scrape away quite a bit in order to extricate Roy from his nest by the time we dropped him at his house at Teets' Corner, just east of Atlanta. We were dead tired when we arrived home at about ten on Christmas Eve with our unwrapped presents under the canvas and a fairly large stack of bills in Dad's pocket. Even so, he never did the Christmas tree lot thing again.

During my growing up years, Dad had set aside an area at the farm which he called the featherbed marsh for my use to cut Christmas trees. Years later, during the mid-seventies, Al Poag and I took our sons, Peter and Joey, to the featherbed marsh to cut a Christmas tree for each of our families. There were several inches of snow on the ground, but my Jeep Wagoneer had no problem on the trail to the marsh. However, after cutting and tying the two trees to its top, the Wagoneer would not start. So we walked out the half-mile to Pleasant Valley Road and the nearest house and called for help. Turns out the snow we kicked up driving in had condensed inside the distributor cap, a not too uncommon cause of car problems in those days.

I ran into Bob Teets a few months ago. "Do you remember when I cut my leg while we were cutting Christmas trees that year?" he asked.

"Sure I do."

"Dumbest thing," he said. "I was trying to stick the axe in a stump and it wasn't staying, so I kicked it."

Remember, it was a double-bitted axe.

STRAIGHT RECKONING

By E. Dan Stevens (2012)

"I think we ought to head over that way," Austin Briley said, pointing to an area where the thick cedar trees seemed to thin out to some extent, letting the sunlight reach the ground in small patches.

"But there's a deer trail heading that way," Harry Dice indicated with a nod of his head.

Larry Wilson was holding his compass. "Yeah, but the lake is in that direction," he said, waving his finger toward an almost impassible thicket halfway between the sunlit ground and the deer trail.

We were one of three or four small groups of Explorer Scouts making our way from the old Clear Lake fire tower to the Twin Tomahawk Lakes campground. There were probably fifteen or sixteen of us in all.

One of the great things about growing up in Atlanta, Michigan, and, I suspect, in many small northern Michigan communities, was that most of our parents, and for that matter most of the adults in the community, were willing to spend time and effort on activities to benefit us kids. A perfect example of this was Colin Wilson, Larry's father. I can't remember if it was his idea or ours, but after we were too old for the regular Boy Scouts, Colin helped us organize an Explorer Scout group for Atlanta. (Although then a distinct branch of scouting for boys over fourteen, the separate Explorer designation has since been discontinued in the U.S. It does continue in England and many other countries.)

It's not that we were that much into the formalities of scouting. If any of us ever earned a merit badge or rose in rank above the entry level, I'm unaware of it. I know that none of us ever bought or wore an Explorer Scout uniform, but there were lots of advantages we did get because we were a recognized group. One was that we got to participate in regional Explorer activities.

For example, a field sports competition was held at the Alpena Fairgrounds one summer. Some seven or eight Explorer posts from northeastern Michigan spent the day competing in events as diverse as softball throwing, log rolling, crosscut log sawing and canoe racing. Our Atlanta team, Robin McMurphy and Bob Teets, won the canoe race, but not without some setbacks along the way. At one point Robin and Bob made a wrong turn after rounding an island and soon noticed that they were passing several canoes - all going in the opposite direction. They quickly recognized their error, turned around, overtook and passed the other canoes - this time in the right direction - and beat them all to the finish line.

I don't recall how long the Atlanta Explorer post was in existence, but I was involved for a year or two. Mr. Wilson liked to periodically have activities for us such as a campout, hike or ice skating party. We would meet at the old V.F.W. Hall, then located next to the Briley Township Park, to plan our next activity. It was there that we decided upon and planned the event that some of us have not forgotten.

Somebody (I don't recall whether it was Mr. Wilson or one of us) suggested that we hike cross-country from the Clear Lake fire tower to the Twin Tomahawk Lakes State Forest campground, a distance of some two and a half miles as the crow flies, and then camp overnight at the campground, and maybe do a little fishing in the lakes. Mr. Wilson volunteered to bring his aluminum boat along for us to use. Everyone became very enthusiastic about the proposed activity, and we decided to do it. We would be able to use our compass and overland navigational skills, and would have a nice camping and fishing trip in the bargain.

The trip was planned for a Saturday in mid-June, 1958. On the Friday evening before, a few of us gathered at Wilson's Grocery to pack our food: hotdogs, buns and pork and beans for Saturday supper (to go with the fish we were going to catch) and bacon and eggs for Sunday breakfast. We packed some marshmallows too. We also took some pop and a couple of gallons of water in old one gallon glass vinegar bottles. The campground had a well with a hand pump and everyone had been instructed to bring sandwiches and a canteen of water for the hike.

Saturday turned out to be a perfect day, sunny and not too hot. We all met at Mr. Wilson's store and tossed our sleeping bags and fishing poles in the back of his pickup. Other parents arrived to drive us out to the fire tower and planned to pick us up the next morning at the lake. By 10:30 am we were all standing at the base of the Clear Lake fire tower.

The Clear Lake fire tower was located on the hill northeast of Clear Lake where the Central Michigan University television tower stands now. It comprised four vertical steel angle pillars at its corners which slanted slightly inward and were strengthened by hundreds of smaller steel angle bars connecting the corner pillar bars. Sitting atop this tower, some sixty feet above the summit of the hill was an observation platform. It was accessible by a staircase constructed within the tower base. From the platform a fire spotter could monitor several thousand acres for smoke and other signs of forest fires. The Twin Tomahawk Lakes were easily visible from the platform to the northeast.

So we all climbed the tower, four or five at a time, and took a compass reading to the lakes, thirty-five degrees east of north. It looked easy. The southern-most lake was only two miles away. Once each of us got our own compass bearing figured out, we scrambled down the tower and set off toward our destination. We didn't plan to travel as one group, but rather as several smaller groups. We were instructed by Mr. Wilson to travel at all times with at least one other person. He saw the last of us off and then drove his pickup with our food and sleeping bags around to the campground to await our arrivals.

The first part of the trek was easy, downhill and through mature oak and red pine trees. Our time estimate of two hours to reach the campground looked like a snap. But guess what? At the bottom of many hill ranges in Montmorency County is a swamp. Such is the case on the northeastern side of the Clear Lake tower hill. Some of the tallest white cedar trees I'd ever seen at that time were in that swamp along with some of the thickest growths of tags and other almost impenetrable spruce groves.

What we didn't realize was that the swamp ran along springs and a small creek that drained into the lakes which were our destination. Since we were following a straight compass course, we were traveling along the length of the swamp all the way to the lakes. Had we followed Austin's idea to head to light or Harry's suggestion to follow the deer trail, we would have reached high ground on either side and could have had an easy hike. As it was, we fought through the swamp for nearly the whole way and didn't reach the campground until late afternoon.

It was too late - and we were too tired - to do any fishing. We ate hot dogs for supper. We had, though, followed a pretty straight compass course to get there.

THE GENERAL STORE

By E. Dan Stevens (2012)

It wasn't the only grocery store in town when I was growing up. Others were Temple's (later Utt's) IGA, Ferguson's Grocery, Trombley's Market, Reiman's Corner, Wilson's Grocery, and the Big Rock Store. But it was more than just a grocery market; it was the general store.

The building was old, probably built by the Cohen brothers in the late teens of the twentieth century. By the time I shopped there during the fifties, the hardwood floors were well worn and many of the aisles sloped a bit due to some obvious settling of foundation and footings. But it was a great store, selling everything from dry goods and shoes to meats and groceries. I actually looked forward to the days when, after school, my mother would give me a list and send me to Peterson's General Store for groceries and whatever else was needed. It was a block from our house.

Peggy (Mrs. Clyde) Brooks remembers when it was owned and operated by brothers, Phil and Harry Cohen, during her early childhood. The winter when her father, John Patrick (Paddy) Hyde, and her whole family was stricken with the flu is what she remembers most about Cohens' store.

"They let us charge our groceries and other necessities for that entire winter as my dad was too sick to work. Not once that I'm aware of did they ever say anything to him about our unpaid bill," Peggy recently told me. "That was a terrible winter. We lived out by Town Corner Lakes. Mary Moggs was kind of like a county nurse going from house to house during that terrible flu epidemic. She would often pick up our groceries from the Cohens' store on her way. I don't know how my mother would have managed without Mary. Also, I was pretty proud when I heard that the Cohens had told others afterward, 'Paddy Hyde paid us back, every cent.'"

Peggy went on to tell me that the Cohens sold the store after a few years and moved to Alpena to operate the Alpena Cigar Co, a maker of fine cigars. (This is not a misprint. Alpena once had at least five cigar manufactures. It even was home to Local 330 of the Cigar Makers' International Union of America. Alpena Cigar Co. brands included the R.K., the El Noble, and the Ship Shape. But I digress.)

The new general store owners were John and Eva Pettenger. John also owned and operated a slaughterhouse near the Boyne City, Gaylord and Alpena Railroad, just east of what is now Pettenger Road on the banks of Hay Meadow Creek. After Gloria Mabie, a grandniece of the Pettengers, told me about them, her son Marty showed me the old slaughterhouse foundations which still exist. John Pettenger operated the general store until the mid-thirties.

After that, Mike Doty and his family owned and operated the general store for the next forty-plus years. It was first known as the M. C. Doty General Store. That changed in the forties to Peterson's General Store when Mike's daughter and son in law, Thelma and Gerald Peterson, took over the business.

But names change hard in Montmorency County. Well into the mid-fifties when I was shopping for my mother, lots of people in Atlanta still called it Doty's. It was pretty confusing to me since Mike Doty's brother, Edgar, still owned and operated Doty Lumber Company across the street.

The sign said Peterson's General Store when I was growing up and it continued to be Peterson's when I returned to Atlanta in 1970. Sometime during the fifties its ownership had changed to Gerald and Thelma's son, Dane, and his wife, Dorothy. But like the name, much of the character of the general store remained the same.

My first memory of anything to do with the general store arrived as part of a bedtime story my father told me about traveling from Kellyville to Atlanta by wagon with his father on Christmas Eve to help buy presents for his eight brothers and one sister. I only remember his reference to the "general store," but it must have been Cohen's or Pettenger's at that time.

Peterson's General Store on right in picture of Atlanta's main street circa 1950

There are lots of other memories, though: going up and down the relatively flat aisles on the east side and newer (sometime after 1935) half of the store with Mother's list where most of the food items were shelved, then back to the meat counter where Dane or Bob Brooks or Mr. Artmolski would weigh and wrap the meat order in white butcher paper and then secure it with string. The price would be written on the package with a black grease pencil.

Usually the list didn't specify items from the dry goods or general merchandise things which were displayed toward the back in the older western part of the store where the floor was noticeably tilted. The checkout counter was at the front on the older side. Bulk flour, sugar and other commodities were located in bins under and behind the checkout counter. It was a counter, no checkout lanes at the general store.

Mrs. (Olive) Burley, Miss (Helen) Carey and Dorothy Peterson were usually behind the counter. I would place my items on the countertop in front of whoever was not busy with another customer. If my mother needed brown sugar or some other bulk item, I would ask for it and then wait while one of the three would record the items and price in the charge book for my family. Some people paid cash, but most local families had a charge book and would pay their grocery bill monthly.

The general store era ended in the spring of 1976. Dorothy Peterson related to me, "Dane and I were returning to Atlanta with another couple. We were coming from the east, somewhere along Beaman and Ruth Smith's farm, when we noticed a red glow ahead. Someone said that it must be the store. And it was."

The following year Vernon Klein built a new building on the same location where he and Marilyn opened and operated a store focused primarily on meats and groceries. Subsequent owners for many years were Bob and Joyce Addis before Bob tragically died in an automobile accident. Its last owners, the Penns, renamed it Penn Station and operated it until it closed a few years ago.

But for me through all the subsequent owners, it was always Peterson's.

THE LAST CAMP

By E. Dan Stevens (2012)

For nearly half a century, from the 1880's through the early 1930's, lumbering camps were the economic engines that brought people and development to Montmorency County, just as they did throughout most of northern Michigan. The "camp" for us was in many ways the economic equivalent of a factory in southern Michigan and New England.

Lumbering camps were in effect temporary villages erected and operated on location to support a particular timbering operation. The typical camp would have at a minimum one or more bunkhouses, a kitchen and dining hall, and a horse barn. Most also had blacksmith and carpenter shops, a camp office, and often some sort of store to serve the lumberjacks, teamsters and other workers who inhabited the camps and labored to harvest and transport the abundant timber resources of early Montmorency and surrounding counties.

Many were the bedtime stories about the camps told to me by my father who grew up in and around such lumbering camps, many of which were operated by his father, George Stevens. Grandfather George came to Atlanta in 1895 and worked as a lumberjack and teamster and then as a foreman and jobber for larger lumbering companies, including Kelly's sawmill in Kellyville and the Kneeland-Bigelow Company, before venturing out on his own sometime in the teen years of the next century.

One of his early camps was on Big Creek west of Lewiston at the very end of the big white pine production years. He also had camps that harvested hardwoods and swamp timber during the teens and twenties. And finally, he operated the last camp, harvesting swamp timber from the late twenties until 1933.

I first visited the site of that last camp when I was eleven or twelve years old with my dad. It was in April, just after the snow had melted and the ground had thawed enough to make most of the old two-rutted roads of northwestern Montmorency County passable. It sort of became a tradition each spring; Dad and I would spend a Sunday afternoon riding around the back roads in some part of the county that was new to me, but familiar to him from his earlier years. Often he would let me drive.

On this particular day, we traveled north on Camp 8 Road, past his sawmill and then through Russell Huff's barnyard and crossed the East Branch of the Black River. We eventually ended up again at the East Branch where the trail ended. Along the way we had crossed the old B.C.G. & A. railroad grade twice and stopped and climbed Old Baldy Hill.

After retracing our route for a mile, or so, Dad instructed me to stop at a small clearing along the edge of the swamp. There had been a spring beside the swamp, he explained, and some cabins which housed lumberjacks and their families. The lumberjacks had worked at Grandfather's last camp which had been on the other side of the half-mile wide band of swamp to our east.

"Do you want to see the old camp site?" he asked.

I answered in the affirmative, so he led me down to the swamp and onto an old corduroy road. It was no longer passable by car or truck as many of the cross-logs had rotted and trees encroached on the roadway, but it was easy enough walking for Dad and me then. (I went back a few years ago and could find no sign of that road.)

"I drove a Model B Ford truck over this road almost every day one summer," he told me, "hauling lumber from the mill and supplies back in. The bridge over the river slanted some and was a little scary, especially since the Model B's mechanical brakes weren't very reliable."

About that time I began to hear the river ahead of us. When we got there, we saw that while the decking of the bridge was gone, the huge logs which spanned the river were still sound and in place. We easily walked across them and on up to the high ground which formed an island in the swamp between the East Branch and Rattlesnake Creek. The old camp had pretty much covered this island.

As Dad and I emerged from the swamp road onto the higher ground of the clearing, an old fence line, most of the posts and some woven wire, still very much evident, extended for several hundred yards southward into a marshy area.

"Pig yard," Dad explained. "The camp raised most of its food. I helped build that fence. In fact, that's where I picked up the rattlesnake while cleaning the debris from a fencepost hole." I'd heard the story many times. "Gave me quite a fright, but no harm done."

Further into the clearing he pointed out the old foundations of the sawmill and its steam engine. A short railroad spur grade ran alongside. Nearby were foundation mounds which outlined the location of many of the camp's buildings. (One of those, the camp office, was moved after the camp closed to Pleasant Valley, fifteen miles east, to become the first marital home for my uncle and aunt, Gayle and Ethyl Stevens.)

A couple of hundred yards north was the main line grade of the B.C.G. & A., running east toward Atlanta and west toward Gaylord. To our right the grade of another spur could be seen. It was more like a sidetrack running parallel to the main line, but was cut into a small knoll which was reinforced with timbers to form a natural loading dock for several cars at a time.

The camp was quite a deal, in many ways like a small town, and even had its own school for the children of its workers. My grandfather himself referred to it in a hot wax record he and my grandmother Gertie made in 1948. "The last job (camp) I had was for Filer Fiber Company of Manistee. Sixteen thousand acres of swamp timber....I had three hundred fifteen men and fifty-five pair of horses, and I looked after them."

After showing me the area where many of the lumberjacks, teamsters and other workers lived north of the tracks, Dad led me back across the swamp on the railroad grade. The old trestle pilings and much of its lower structure were still intact and we easily crossed the river as we made our way to the car.

I don't remember all that Dad told and showed me that day as we toured the site of so much activity some twenty-five years earlier, but most of the details have stuck with me through the intervening years, and I have since learned quite a bit more about Grandfather's last camp.

Over the years since I have visited the old camp site many times, but have come to regret one time when I didn't.

As a young man, Ken Chadwick, later to be longtime Montmorency County Register of Deeds, had taught at the camp's schoolhouse for a few years, with and then succeeding his mother, Laura Crank. (Claude Mowery had also been the teacher there for a least a year.)

During the mid-eighties, Ken on several occasions talked to me about his days as a teacher there and suggested that we go together sometime to the old campsite. He wanted to revisit the site and also to show me where the schoolhouse and other buildings had been located.

Since Ken was then retired and I was busy with my law practice, he left it to me to pick a time, indicating that he would likely be available whenever it was convenient for me. Sadly, as you might guess, I kept putting it off and putting it off until it was too late.

I've heard many stories from uncles and others who worked or visited the camp. Uncle Doc (Arno) told of the time he and Uncles Burl and Avon were supposed to be loading some rail cars for the next train, but got sidetracked by some friends who stopped by. When they finally got back to their jobs, it was getting dark. By the time they finished it was midnight.

"Luckily there was some moonlight," he told me. "I don't know if we were more scared of falling off the cars or of what Dad would say to us if they weren't loaded for the next day's train."

Uncle Olin, younger than Burl, Doc and Avon, had worked in the kitchen and dining hall.

Oral McMurphy recently told me about going with his father to visit his Aunt Frances and her husband, Bill Lucas, who were the camp cooks.

"Naturally we would stay to eat," he said. "I remember one of the rules at the table was no 'short-stopping' on passed food without permission from the person requesting that the food be passed. We had the same rule at Army camps during World War II. There was always a cigar box full of toothpicks for the lumberjacks by the door of the dining shack.

"I can also remember liking to look at all of the teams in the horse barn. But best of all was the game I played with the boys who lived at the camp," Oral told me. "We would go across the river on the corduroy road to Old Baldy Hill and push an old truck tire to the top and let it roll. It was a long climb up the hill, but the tire would go a long way if it didn't hit a tree."

Over the years, I have run into many people who remembered the camp. While campaigning in 1974 for my first term in the Legislature, I stopped at the Sparr Store to introduce myself and leave some literature promoting my candidacy. An elderly customer upon hearing my name asked if I had been related to George Stevens. The rest of our conversation went something like this:

"Yes," said I, "he was my grandfather."

"Well, let me shake your hand," he said, "and give me a bundle of your brochures to pass out to my friends. I worked for your grandfather at his camp in the swamp. He was a good man and kept many of us around here working through the worst part of the depression."

A few years later in Boyne City, Art Rouse introduced me to a gentleman named Ray Garlinghouse. Mr. Garlinghouse asked if I was related to Bud Stevens and George Stevens. I explained that George Stevens was my grandfather and that Bud (Harold), my uncle, was his oldest son.

Ray Garlinghouse, then in his eighties, went on to tell me that he had been an engineer for the B.C.G. & A. Railroad for many years. "We stopped running trains between Gaylord and Alpena in 1929 or 1930, but that didn't last long because of your grandfather's operations in the swamp. We reopened the line as far as Atlanta just to serve his lumber camp.

"I would regularly pull thirteen empty flat cars and sometimes a box car from Gaylord to the Stevens Camp. We would drop them there and then run the engine on to Atlanta where we would turn it around on the wye just east of the Atlanta Depot. We'd pull back in front of the closed depot and then bank the engine fires for the night.

"The fireman and I would walk the few block's to your Uncle Bud's hotel where we would have dinner and stay the night. After breakfast we would head back to the engine. I got to know Bud Stevens pretty good during those years.

"After opening the drafts and getting up steam, we would run back to the Stevens Camp and pick up the loads from the previous several days, usually about thirteen, and then head on toward Gaylord. We would sometimes drop a car or two at Gaylord for interchange with the Michigan Central (Railroad), but most we would haul all the way to Boyne Falls for interchange with the G.R.& I (Grand Rapids and Indiana Railroad). The Gaylord cars were usually lumber, tamarack poles for fishnet stakes, and some of the cedar for fence posts. The balsam, spruce and poplar cordwood and cedar for ties went on to the Boyne City interchange, most of it bound for Manistee.

"This went on into 1933 when the Stevens Camp closed. After that, B.C.G. & A. trains stopped running east of Gaylord," Ray concluded, "but I worked for the railroad many years after and was still an engineer when it only traveled from Boyne City to Boyne Falls, and we switched from steam to diesel."

I have recently become acquainted with Bob Polidan of Manistee whose grandfather, Ed "Rascal" Hart, had worked for a few years at the camp. Rascal spent much of his life as a hunter, trapper and lumberjack in the Black River area and loved to tell his grandson about his experiences. He also knew and sang for Bob a number of folk songs originating from trapper shacks and lumber camps. Rascal was a front line lumberjack, cutting trees with an axe and crosscut saw. Among his friends at the Stevens Camp was a character named Green Eyed Mike. He also recalled and related to Bob that several Native Americans worked at the camp, most with specialized skills such as saw filing and the like.

Bob recalls that his grandfather had often referred to it as the Rattlesnake Camp. On my Uncle Arno's (Doc) EARLY DAYS IN MONTMORENCY COUNTY MAP, it is called the "Stevens Black River Camp." My father always referred to it as, "Dad's last camp."

While most of the people who worked at or visited the camp during its operations have passed on, and I know of it only from stories, I do have at my cabin a Montmorency County map from the 1930's. Prominent on it along the B.C.G. & A. Railroad in Vienna Township is a community dot simply labeled, "Stevens."

THE HOUSE

By E. Dan Stevens (2013)

"Were you sad about your old house?" This question in one form or another was put to me quite often during the past few months. It had been in disrepair for the past several years, a state hard to hide because of its location on the main street of Atlanta, between the hardware store and the real estate office. It housed a real estate office (mine) itself during the 70's, and later was a doctor's clinic. But mostly I remember it as the house where I grew up. They tore it down this past summer. And yes, I was sad about it.

During its hundred plus years of existence, the house has been the home of two state legislators, three Postmasters, three owners of the Atlanta Hardware, and a Sargent-at-Arms of the Michigan Senate.

It was built by Grove Rouse sometime around the turn of the century, the one before last. Mr Rouse owned and operated the hardware store and post office next door. He was also, among many other things, a partner with my grandfather in several lumbering ventures. Originally a one-story, the house was expanded by at least two additions during its years as the Rouse home. Their children, Mattie and Spike, lived there during childhood. Spike would later become the Montmorency County Road Commission Engineer.

When Grove Rouse left Atlanta during the 20's to become a Senate official in Lansing, the hardware store and house were sold to Hans Briley who also became the Atlanta Postmaster. Along the way Hans' oldest son,

The house in June, 2013, a few days before demolition began

Mattie Rouse (later Mattie Price) standing in front of the then single story house in 1911

Carl, took over the hardware store and Waldo Whitehead became the Postmaster. In 1936 Waldo moved the post office from the hardware store to its first stand-alone site in a building located between Doty Lumber Company and Goldie's Grill. K D Custom Interiors is located at that site today.

Waldo and Helen Whitehead purchased and moved into the house with their two children, Gloria and Gary, just before the start of World War II.

My parents, Ross and Rose Stevens, bought the house from the Whiteheads in November, 1952, when I was nine and we lived there until I was almost out of college. It was the home of my youth, the place where I grew up, and integral to all of my experiences during those years and my memories of them today. Years later, as an adult, I purchased it and again lived there for a brief time and for longer used it for business purposes.

The house itself was a structure of substance. The original part had a two inch thick sub-floor supported by pine log beams, all clearly visible from the full basement. The floor boards comprised 2 x 12s and wider rough-sawed white pine planks twenty or more feet in length, readily available in northern Michigan at the time of the original construction.

The first addition (evident in a picture of Mattie Rouse taken about 1911) included a kitchen and an inside bathroom, but not a basement. It did have a large cistern under the kitchen which could be seen from the crawlspace. The floor construction of this addition was joist and one-inch thick sub-floor.

A later addition or additions added a second floor in two parts, one over the original house with two bedrooms, and another over the first addition with one bedroom and an unfinished storage area. Also, probably at the time of the second story addition, a large pillared porch was added across the entire front of the original structure.

Two additional structures were in the back yard. The two car garage was probably constructed at the same time as the original house because it had a plank floor suitable for carriages and other horse drawn vehicles, but not strong enough for modern automobiles. We used it mostly for storage, but one year I raised two calves in the garage, feeding them a calf formula until the snow had melted and they were large enough to fend for themselves at my dad's farm.

The other building was my clubhouse. Not originally, of course; it was built to house water pumps and a Delco unit for the house and hardware store. Half of the structure was below grade level and half was above.

Access was by a stair going down three feet or so to the floor. It was about twelve feet by sixteen feet in size. The walls were concrete and brick, and the roof was reinforced concrete with only a slight pitch. We used it as a stage for neighborhood plays and the like.

None of the machinery remained when my friends and I used it for our activities, but the large blocks upon which the generator and pumps and tanks had been mounted were still there. We used them for tables and benches. Also, two three-inch well casings remained. We could drop pebbles down and hear water splashing.

A number of pipes intruded from the walls toward the house and hardware building, another toward the street. I remember hearing once that Grove Rouse had installed fire hydrants at the corners of the lot and next to the store which connected to some of the pipes.

The house itself was not only constructed of materials no longer available today, but it had a number of features which combined to make it a comfortable place to live. It had a steam heating system with big cast iron radiators in every room. The steam valves released just enough steam from each radiator to effect an agreeable level of humidity throughout. One of the radiators was under a large window diagonally overlooking the corner and the main street activities of downtown. (During the 50s there were no street signs and none of us knew that what we referred to as "main street" was actually named State Street on the town Plat.) Whenever I was house-ridden because of weather or illness, I would put pillows on the radiator and watch the activities of downtown.

The original coal-fired steam boiler cracked sometime during the 40's and was replaced by a new fuel oil boiler. Gloria Mabie (then Gloria Whitehead) told me that she and her brother Gary had been told by their father of steps to take if the boiler ever failed. She recalls that they opened the basement door and found the basement full of steam, and that they ran down the stairs to close the valves and damper as they had been instructed.

There are, of course, many incidents which I recall that occurred over the years in the house, such as getting caught by Mrs. Violet Blamer, who owned the telephone company, when I spliced my own extension crank telephone to the phone wire running through the basement (my parents didn't know until she called them,) and playing basketball down there with the basket being a space between a steam pipe and the house floor. (How was I to know that wearing off the pipe insulation with the basketball was not cool?) Come to think of it, those things that didn't exactly work out right do stand out in my mind, maybe because of the punishment they engendered. On the other hand, one learned a lot too. For example if I disconnected the ringer, Mrs. Blamer couldn't tell when I spliced another phone onto the line.

Did I mention location? For a boy growing up, there could not have been a better location in Atlanta. Across the side street was Tunnicliff's Drug Store. Across the main street was Utt's Shell Station and Café (later purchased and operated by the Pinchocks and Hamiltons.) Both the drug store and café had soda fountains; the drug store had better chocolate sodas (25¢) and sundaes (30¢), but Utt's had better malted milk shakes (30¢) and banana splits (35¢). I didn't very often have enough money for these things, but when I did, watch out. I also recall that the drug store received the new Saturday Evening Post (15¢) edition every Tuesday. I could usually talk my mother into giving me the 15 cents because she liked to read it too.

Briley's Atlanta Hardware next door and Erity's Sport Shop two doors past the drug store were great places to browse and buy B-Bs and roller skate keys when you needed them. Did I tell you about Goldie's (Irons) Grill sugar donuts (5¢) only a block away? Still the best donuts I have ever eaten.

PART II

     During the seven or eight years the Cant Hardly Tales appeared in the Montmorecy County Tribune, then Publisher Jim Young suggested that I invite others to contribute to the column. I did and they did. Unfortunately, page restrictions do not allow all of those stories submitted and published in the column to be included in this book, but several are included and I will provide electronic copies of the tales which are not republished in this book upon request made to *canthardly@yahoo.com*.

     The stories which follow are by Doug King of Lewiston, Julie Marsh Mowery of Vienna Township, Betty Powell Wright of Hillman, Craig Sherwood of Atlanta (submitted by his daughter, Claudia), Francis Vondette Fritzs of Bay City and Sue Gavine Weaver of Atlanta. Other contributors were Ernie Paul and Barry Danks.

LIFE IN THE OLD COURTHOUSE

By Betty Powell Wright (2016)

The Montmorency County Sheriff and his family in the early 1940's lived in the County Courthouse. My father, Martin Powell, Sr., was the Sheriff. I was nearing my teen years when we moved into the old Courthouse.

One end of the building contained the living quarters of the Sheriff and the female and male jails. The male jail was in the basement area off the dining room. The female jail was on the second floor between my parent's bedroom and the county offices. There were three more bedrooms on the third floor. The only bathroom for the sheriff's quarters was in the basement. There was a kitchen and living room in the basement also.

The sheriff had many duties. He was custodian and grounds keeper in addition to his law duties. My older sister, Naomi, and brother, Eugene, helped him with the custodian duties. Every office had a spittoon. Each night my father would clean them with a brush and hose. Naomi would empty all the waste baskets and helped my father and brother sweep the offices and large hallway. My brother, Martin Jr., and myself were forbidden to go into any of the offices but our fathers.

The courthouse was closed on Saturdays. My brother Martin and I would sometimes go up to the courtroom on the third floor and pretend we were the judges.

The sheriff issued the drivers license. My mother was made deputy which enabled her to issue drivers licenses if my father was busy. She also provided three meals a day for the prisoners and kept the bedding for them clean. It was my fathers job to also keep the jails clean. During his time in office he did not have a female prisoner.

There was at one time a certain young man serving time in the jail for a period of two months. Often when my father was around he would allow the young man, our only prisoner then, out for exercise and to do light maintenance jobs. On Sunday when we attended church he would go with us. If we did not have company, my mother would often invite him to eat at our table. He was very polite and always wanted to help.

The jail, I thought, was smelly. My mother kept things very clean, but it was old. The young prisoner was very grateful and expressed his thanks often for the kindness and trust.

When his time was served he again expressed thanks and we said our goodbyes. We missed him. About a month after his release we found him knocking on our door. He told my mother that he came to show us his new car. We went out and looked it over. He told us he had a job and was doing well. He asked us to go for a ride in his new car. Mother, my sister Naomi, my brother Martin, Jr. and I all climbed in. We were very excited and happy for him. We reached the edge of Atlanta village limits and headed on M-32 toward Hillman.

Suddenly there were flashing lights behind us. I looked out the rear window to see my father's car coming. We immediately pulled over to the side of the road. My father parked in back of us and walked up to the driver's side. I could hear him say something about a stolen car to the driver who he recognized.

Then he looked into the car at the passengers. I will never forget the surprised look on his face. The driver (I shall not mention his name) just broke out with laughter. The car had been reported as stolen and the Sheriff found his own family in the car with the man accused of stealing it.

No charges of stealing the car were ever filed though as the ex-prisoner had conspired with the car's owner to play this joke on my father.

Living in the Courthouse as a child was a fun and exciting experience. It was close to where my friends lived. Geraldine Briley was across the street. Kathleen Mowery was on the corner and Virgina (don't recall her last name), daughter of the minister of the Congregational Church, was on the main street. One hot day we decided to have a lemonade stand. We decided at the end of the sidewalk leading to the front door of the courthouse would be a good place. Our business was doing well until my father came out to tell us we would have to move.

Sidney Gassel, the Prosecuting Attorney, had to share an office. He wanted his own office. It was decided that the Sheriff's bedroom could be divided to create a separate office for Mr. Gassel. One of our favorite places to play was under a big tree beside the Courthouse. It happened to be right under the window of Sidney Gassel's new office. Sidney yelled out several times telling us we were too noisy.

Finally my father told us we could not play in that area during office hours. The railing on the steps going to the front door of the courthouse was a metal pole. It was fun to slide down the pole. My father again said that it was off limits during office hours.

When winter came it was so convenient for ice skating on the Thunder Bay River next to the Courthouse. Eugene would clean an area and build a fire. Someone gave me a pair of skates. They were black and too large but I stuffed the toes to make them fit. We always were given one gift of choice for Christmas and I wore out the catalog looking at pretty white skates. For Christmas I got them.

January, 1942, arrived. It was a Saturday. My mother had just given birth to our brother Charles. My sister noticed flickering outside on the snow. Dad went out to see what was making it. He ran back in to tell us the cupola was on fire. The courthouse burned to the ground. My ice skates burned. People cried. I cried too. I lost my fun place to live and play and my ice skates.

Living in the Courthouse was an experience I will always cherish.

POWELL AND McCOY
BLUNDERS

By Betty Powell Wright (2009)

Eugene Powell, my brother, loved airplanes while growing up in Atlanta, Michigan, during the 30's and 40's. He was eight years older, but I always remember his room. Everywhere strings extended from the ceiling with model airplanes hanging from the them. Money that he would earn doing odd chores was always spent on airplane kits and he spent every free hour putting together.

When he was about fourteen he decided that he would build a big plane that would have skis and would go down the sliding snow hill. He collected the materials needed. An old steering wheel, pair of skis, wood, cardboard and canvas. He spent every free moment that summer working on this plane. It was a one person plane. Big enough to sit in with wings, tail and a place in front where an engine would be. (Of course the only power was gravity and the skis.)

My younger brother and I were forbidden to go in the garage where his plane was. I would sneak looks through the window and when he wasn't around I would go in the garage and really look his project over. I sometimes would dream that perhaps he would allow me to drive it down the hill.

Some of the kids that slid down the hill heard about his project and kept asking when it would be finished and ready to go. The hill was on

Pettenger Road. The hill was fairly steep and gradually went down to Hay Meadow Creek. (Today the hill no longer exists. They have cut the hill down and changed the whole terrain.) Eugene spent hours working on the hill, clearing back the brush and smoothing out the bottom that went on to the creek.

I could hardly wait for the day when he would go down the hill. It was really a very neat plane, all framed in with wood and covered with cardboard and then canvas. It had a door and a seat for the pilot. The windshield was open. It had a stick on the floor. (I think it was the brake.) He had it all painted red and black.

We had a great snow fall that winter and finally one Sunday in February he announced that he would be going down the hill the next Saturday. I could hardly wait. I told some of my friends and Eugene told some of his friends. Our family, with camera in hand, all marched to the hill and watched while the plane was taken out of the garage and pulled by a rope up to the top.

Eugene posed with a pair of goggles beside his plane while we took a picture. (The picture was later destroyed in the courthouse fire. We lived there at the time of the fire. It was one of the things that I felt very bad about losing.) Eugene climbed in. His friends gave him a push. We all clapped, held our breath and down the hill he went.

I don't know what happened. Maybe the brake didn't work or maybe it was the steering wheel. Close to the very bottom of the hill it veered off and hit a tree. Eugene did not get hurt but his plane was a total loss. He did not wish to talk about it. He pulled it home and burned it.

When he was drafted into the army later in life he became a pilot.

Some years later as young adults, Eugene and our sister Naomi's husband, Jack McCoy, Sr., loved to fish together. They did not own a boat and had to rent one or borrow one whenever they went fishing. Eugene drew up some plans for building a boat and took them over for his brother-in-law, Jack, to look over. Jack thought they were good. He suggested that perhaps they could build it together.

Neither of them at that time had a garage. Jack had a basement, however, and suggested that they build it there. Idea sounded good to Eugene. Money at that time was a little tight as they had small children and had not been out of the military very long. They made up a list of all the needed materials and bought them as money became available.

They worked all winter on their boat. Their goal was to have it completed for spring fishing. April came and the boat was done. All sanded, painted and it even had cushions to sit on. They bought oars and a small motor. They told their wives, Naomi and Violet, they were ready for fishing and to get the fry pan ready.

They carried the boat to the bottom of the stairs. Wow! Boat was too large. They tugged and pushed, turned and twisted upside and down but they could not get the boat up the stairs. They sat down on the bottom step and laughed. All that work, all that money. They decided to take the boat apart move it to the yard and put it back together.

I only heard the story. I never got to see the boat. I think it did get taken apart and removed from the basement because Naomi wanted the room it took up, but I don't think it ever got put back together again.

HUNTING COWS

By Francis Vondette Fritzs (2009)

At the age of fourteen my father, James Vondett, arrived in Lewiston with his eighteen year old brother, Edward, to work in the mills. Sixteen year old Marie came to keep house for them and teach in a rural school. Ten year old Pearl came to keep her company.

The next summer, June 1904, the rest of the family came. John and Elizabeth Vondett and seven year old Beth rode in a covered wagon, with the chickens tied in cages on the sides. Grandpa Edward herded the cattle all the way from their farm in Saginaw County. It was a two-week trip. They arrived in Lewiston and bought farm land at the corner of what is now County Road 612 and Avery Lake Road. They had 120 acres of cut-over land that little Beth said grew nothing but stones and pine stumps.

My father loved the farm. He married, raised a family, and farmed there until his death in 1962.

When I was a child in the 1920's, County Road 612 didn't exist. There was just a dirt road that ended in the swamp a mile east of our house. There was a wagon trail that went over the hills, past Avery Lake on its way to Atlanta. Another trail went to Comins. There were also old logging trails and cow paths wandering through the woods.

Our farm was the last one in the community. There was lots of state land and most of the farmers turned their cows out in the morning to fend for themselves. Older children had the job of going out late in the afternoon to "hunt the cows" and bring them home for milking.

The summer when I was nine I shared the job with my twelve year old sister. When I was ten the job of "hunting cows" was mine alone. My only company was our old collie, Pal, who spent most of the time off chasing rabbits.

I was terrified to be alone in the woods. I wouldn't believe there were no dangerous animals. There were so many different noises to startle me as little animals skittered about. Once I was so scared I couldn't even yell, when a tiny fawn bleated and took off from where his mother had hidden him in the tall grass. I had nearly stepped on it.

The area had lots of grassy meadows and places for the cows to get a drink withing a mile or two from our home, but I never knew which place they would choose to go. I learned early on how to look for fresh tracks and how to listen for the cow bells. Each farmer strapped a bell on the necks of three or four of his cows. The bells were all different tones and I soon learned to identify herds by the sound of their bells. The herds seldom mingled and one rarely came across a neighbor out "hunting cows."

A little over a mile northwest of our farm was Moss Lake. To the north of that was a stream flowing across a meadow where the grass was abundant. About two miles north of our home was a creek flowing into Avery Lake. There was another creek flowing out of a swamp east of Avery Lake. About a mile from home was a big meadow with a spring fed water hole. That was a favorite place for both me and the cows, so I always went there first. A mile east of that was a creek flowing into Sage Lake. Turning toward the south came Hunt Creek, Fish Creek and Fish Lake. The creeks all had a tin cup hanging near the trail so a traveler could stop for an ice cold drink.

All of these watering places were about two miles from home. If I didn't find the cows at one, I had to walk on to another. I always left home at four o'clock, rain or shine. Sometimes I was lucky and found the cows right away; other times, I had quite a hike. Other times, it was nearly dark when I gave up and went home empty-handed.

It never made my folks happy when I came home without the cows. Though the cows usually wandered home during the night, they had missed a milking. This wasn't good for them or our cream pay check. Dad shipped cans of sour cream every week by truck to Bay City. That was our only source of income during the summer months.

I had five years of "cow hunting" before my brother, Henry, was old enough to take over the job. By then I had a vast knowledge of nature.

I had learned to identify the trees, flowers, birds and animals and developed a love for hiking. Those terrifying early years had not been wasted.

Once on a visit to the Vondett farm when my girls were young adults, I thought it would be fun to show them where I use to "hunt cows". We were all good hikers, but by the time we had covered half the circle and come to County Road 612 I found a shady tree to sit under. They then hiked another mile to get a car and came back to pick me up. I found I had lost a lot of my youthful energy.

November, 2009 Note: I received this story a few weeks ago along with the following letter from Mrs. Fritzs:
"Dear Mr. Stevens,
I surely enjoy the "Can't Hardly" articles in Montmorency County Tribune. I'm an old timer, will soon be 89, and so the stories stir up many memories for me. I'm sending you a memory from my childhood that astounds my relatives of today. No one would think of giving a ten year old girl such a task today.
Frances Vondett Fritzs
New Baltimore, Michigan"

I wanted to add some more background on Mrs. Fritzs and called her home on November 29th and spoke with her daughter, Linda. I did learn that she attended the Lewiston School through the tenth grade and then went to live with an aunt downstate to finish high school. I also learned that the farm at the corner of 612 and Avery Lake Road remains in her family and is frequently visited by them.

Sadly, Linda also informed me that her mother had passed away after a brief illness the night before. I had never met nor talked to Francis Vondett Fritzs, but reading this well-written and descriptive tale of her childhood chore makes me wish I could have known her. - Dan Stevens

GROWING UP NEXT TO THE BIG BARN

By Julie Marsh Mowery (2009)

I was probably too young to remember my first glimpse of the barn, but I imagine that even then I must have been as wowed as nearly everyone else seemed to be at first sight. "It fills the valley!" and "It takes your breath away!" and "I had no idea it was that huge!" were common exclamations by friends visiting my home at the former K-B Farm for the first time. They were referring to what in those days was called "The K-B Barn" or "The Big Barn" or simply "The Barn," the most prominent feature to meet one's eye upon driving into the valley where we lived.

In October, 1948, my parents, Harry and Faye Marsh, purchased 1,700 plus acres in Briley and Vienna Townships of Montmorency County. The property included the fields and buildings of what during the 1920's had been known as the Aberdeen Farm. By far the most impressive of the buildings was the barn.

The Aberdeen Farm was owned and operated by The Kneeland-Bigelow Company, a major timber operator in Montmorency County and other parts of northern Michigan for the first three decades of the last century. The farm's primary purpose was to supply meat, dairy and poultry products for the lumberjacks working at the company's several lumber camps in the area.

The barn was built in 1920 by John Harrington of Gaylord. It was designed to be a show place as well as a functional, working barn. I have been told that it was planned to be one foot longer than the longest, one

**The people and wagon at the doors of the Kneeland-Biglow Barn
provide perspective as to its size**

foot wider than the widest, and one foot taller than the tallest barns in
Michigan. In other words, it was the biggest barn in the state when built.
It also contained many of the most modern operational characteristics for
barns at that time.

According to Herman Lunden Miller in his book, *Lumbering in
Early Twentieth Century Michigan, The Kneeland-Bigelow Experience,* the
barn measured 66 feet wide by 160 feet long and was 80 feet high from
basement floor to roof, including a basement ceiling height of 9 feet. The
cupola was 18 feet high and 24 feet wide and extended the entire length of
the barn. Galvanized steel vents were added to the cupola in 1921 and
were connected by ducts to the basement. (One of these vents is located
at the Montmorency County Fair Grounds.) The floor of the barn had
litter carriers so the liquid manure would drain off into a pit at the south
end of the barn.

I was four years old and my sister, Elaine, was two years old when
we moved to the caretaker's house on our new property. Glenn, my

brother, was born there in 1949. In 1950 we moved to the big house closer to the barn. My brother Harley was born in 1951.

It was a wonderful place to grow up. There were many interesting buildings. There were the caretaker's house, little well house (both are still there), horse barn and blacksmith shop. On the corner there was an office building, then the bunkhouse, the big house - and the Big Barn. Behind the barn there were a pig house, smokehouse and a slaughter house. At the end of the pig house was a flowing well. The silos located behind the barn were gone when we moved there; all that was left were the cement bottoms. On top of the big hill behind the barn were two water reservoirs. The hill was one of the places where we spent much of our time. In the summer it was a great place to hang out and feel like you were on top of the world; in the winter it was a great sledding hill.

The big house did not have electricity when we moved in so we used gas lanterns for lights. Our water came from a pitcher pump in the kitchen sink. There was a well house behind the big house and later when we had electricity we would run a hose in through the window to fill the reservoir on the wood cook stove. My mother cooked on the wood stove and we had an ice box to keep our perishables cold. We took baths in a galvanized tub behind the cook stove, always one of the warmest places in the house. As kids we thought we were rich, not just because of where we lived, but also because we had two outhouses.

My parents raised sheep, pigs, chickens, turkeys and dairy cows. We milked cows and separated the milk and sold the cream. They also grew yellow eyed beans, oats and hay. My mother always had a garden and canned our food from her garden. She sold eggs and at Thanksgiving she sold freshly dressed turkeys. In the spring we tapped maple trees and made maple syrup. We had a team of Percherons that we used to gather the sap.

When my father would go to the feed store, located across the road from the Big Rock Store, to purchase feed for the animals, my sister and I would go with him so we could pick out the feed bags we liked as my mother would make our dresses from these. She also made her dish towels from the feed bags.

Several irons were kept on the wood stove. When ironing a removable handle would be detached from an iron that had cooled and reattached to a hot one. Sometimes in the winter, Mother wrapped irons in a towel and put them in our beds to keep us warm.

I can not imagine growing up anywhere else; it was lots of work, but much more fun. We all have many wonderful memories or our time spent at the K-B Barn. Many of our friends still talk of the great times they had there. We were the only children to ever live there.

My family lived there until 1956 when my father moved the bunkhouse up to the property in Vienna Township on M-32 just north of Deadman's corner. He then added on to this and built the house we always call the red house. This house is still there, but is vacant.

Because of rising taxes and decreasing farm profits, my family could not afford to keep all of the property. We pared down to 320 acres in Section 13, Vienna Township, on which was located the red house, our home throughout the remaining of my school years.

A subsequent owner of the Briley Township property, which included the Big Barn, tore it down a few years later. It was very sad for me, having grown up in its shadow, to see it go.

A BARN DANCE ...
"Do-Sa-Do and Allemande Left"
(1921 -1929)

By Douglas A. (Dugal) King (2010)

Charles Dickens had it right in his novel, <u>The Tale of Two Cities</u>: "It was the best of times...it was the worst of times...." This is a true story of events during the roaring 20's in rural Montmorency County, Michigan.

My parents, Gordon and Ruby King, were hacking out a living on an eighty acre parcel of land four miles north of Lewiston on County Rd 491. They had been married on Thanksgiving Day, November 25, 1921. By the time the summer of 1928 rolled around, they had started a family of two girls; Lyllis, born in 1924, and Thelma, born in 1925. I did not show up until later in the saga. They had built a four room "palace" out of rough-sawn lumber. The roof was covered with tarpaper. The outside walls were also covered with tarpaper with nailed strips of lath to keep the tar paper from being blown away. Those were the days of farming with horses. Tractors had been invented by John Deere, Ford, Huber and others, but none had yet arrived in Montmorency County.

They had harvested the hay for the winter by late July, and the only field left was a five-acre parcel of green oats. They decided not to wait for the oats to ripen and were going to harvest the oats for feed as soon as they dried in the field. They were down to the last load in the field and were hurrying to get the full load to the barn before a threatening thunderstorm would overtake them. The storm was rapidly developing in the southwestern sky. My mother was building the load on the wagon as my Dad pitched the bundles up to her with a three-tined pitchfork. The last load was a torture for her because she was wearing a housedress...(jeans for women had not been invented yet)...and as the load grew, so did her Scottish temper.

She exclaimed to Dad, "These d*** thistles. The only thing they are good for is burning."

Finally the last bundle was on the wagon and they headed for the barn. When they got there, my mother took off for the house to start the noon meal. Lyllis and Thelma trotted along with her, as they had been along on the haying project as was often done in those days. My dad was gong to unhook the team of horses. He had done that and was sitting on the edge of the hay mow watching the heavy downpour through the open barn door. Their collie dog, Spark, sat beside him.

One of the horses, Nip, was munching hay from the mow and stood between the open door and Dad. That probably saved Dad's life because that is when the lightning struck the barn. The strike apparently hit the barn doors track. It knocked the horse down before striking my Dad and knocking him unconscious. He related in later years that the last thing he remembered was a ball of fire the size of his fist coming at him and shaking him like a dog shaking a rat. When he came to, smoke and flickering flames were coming up through the hay in the mow. He tried to smother the flames with hay to no avail. He tried to stand up but couldn't. He crawled past the horse, which at the time he thought to be dead, got outside and screamed for help. He pulled the wagon from the barn and also the grain binder, which later took three men to move. Neighbors showed up to help, but too late. The barn was a total loss.

My sister Thelma remembers standing with my mother at the front door of the house and seeing the smoke billowing from the barn as it drifted northeastward in the darkened sky. Edna (Newell) Mattison, who would have been five or six then, remembers the same smoke and her mother Hilder saying , "Oh my God, they are losing their barn."

The barn was a goner as was the winter's feed for the livestock. Spark, the collie, ran away and was gone for three days. The horse, Nip, apparently came to and got out of the barn on his own. For the rest of their lives, Nip, Spark and Dad all stayed inside during thunderstorms whenever they could. Dad would lie down on a bed, Spark would crawl under the bed, and Nip would stand in his stall in the new barn with his ears laid back and his legs trembling.

The good news was that they had insurance on the barn. However, the claim dragged on for quite some time. In the meantime, they decided to proceed with building a new barn. This is where the time frame gets a little fuzzy for me. The barn was finished in the late summer of 1929. I was born January 21, 1929.

Greg Sutter of Gaylord was a renowned barn builder of that era. He was a master craftsman in building timber barns which is no longer done. He gave my Dad a list of materials that would be needed to build a structure 60' x 70' and 50' in height. The new barn would have two sliding doors at the entrance of the hay loft area. There was a hay mow area on each side of the up stairs entrance. A track in the peak ran the length of the barn and was rigged with a system of pulleys and 200' of one-inch rope. It provided a means of unloading hay from a wagon with a grapple hayfork. This eliminated the task of unloading the wagon with a pitchfork. An area below the hay mow floor sheltered non-stanchioned farm animals during inclement weather.

Dad and my uncle, Les King, spent the winter of 1928 cutting logs to be sawn in the spring. I am guessing it was my grandfather, James Proper, who sawed these logs into suitable materials for the builder's specifications. He had a steam engine, a sawmill, and also a threshing machine. Some of the logs were pine, but most of the main timbers were from hard maple, beech or hemlock.

Quite a few of the timbers in the barn show signs of being hand hewn with a broad-ax. Mr. Sutter spent the better part of the summer fitting timbers with his hand tools, whittling pegs to hold timbers together where the holes had been bored with a ship auger. Sutter had many visitors as he worked.

One observer asked him as he was backing a ship auger out of a timber, "Where is your blueprint?"

He smiled, knocked the shavings from the auger, and said, "Do you see that hole? That is my blue print."

Once Mr. Sutter had finished cutting and drilling the rafters and other timbers to fit, and the basement walls had been poured by Newt and Bud Cahoon, my parents set the date for a barn raising bee.

Edna Mattison told me with a laugh, "I remember them bringing the piano for the barn dance down from Sylvester King's house on an old flat-bed truck. As they slowly went by the our (Newell) farm, Vance Putman, Sr., was sitting on the piano stool playing some tune of the times."

On the morning of the selected date, dawn broke to a drizzling rain and fog. The volunteer crew of 40 men, with their hand tools, arrived by 8:00 AM. By that time the rain had stopped, and the work began in earnest. There must have been great teamwork and great organizational skills shown that day because before nightfall the barn was up. A barn dance was planned for that evening to celebrate the accomplishment.

All of this has been related to me over the years as I was just a baby at the time, being born in the winter of 1929. They told me that Wayne Winter and I slept in the same crib at the barn dance that evening. Vance Putman and Dutch Winter took turns calling square dances and Lelia Winter played the piano. Old Joe Cauchon played the fiddle. What other musicians they had that evening, I do not know.

Many good people helped the day of the barn raising.. Bud Cahoon told me that he and Chuck Kuivininen, both teenagers at the time, did the major part of erecting the rafters during that stage of the construction. I am guessing that other members of the crew were Newt Cahoon, Jake Sherbonda, Eric Agren, Ed Hermanson, Charlie Newell, John Newell, Skinny Newell, Dutch Winter, Vance Putman Sr., Dell Putman, Guy Ellsworth, Lyle Mowery, Frank Smith, Sylvester King and Art King. There were many others.

There were also lots of women preparing food for the workers. It must have been a glorious affair. The barn still stands today. It is on the west side of County Road 491. It is an example of pioneer workmanship, cooperation by caring people, perseverance of a young couple, and the ability to overcome adversity. It is a shining example of the rural American spirit.

Doug King and the barn erected at the 1929 barn-raising bee as seen from County Road 491 north of Lewiston

RECOLLECTIONS OF MY GRANDFATHER, SYLVESTER S. KING

By Douglas A. King (2002)

At the urging of Dave King, my son, and my sister, Thelma Sawyer, I am going to relate my early memories and impressions of my grandfather. I cannot remember the exact dates of most of these flashbacks; the few dates included will probably only be close.

Sylvester S. King was born in Old Deer Shire, Aberdeen, Scotland, October 29, 1864. He died January 29, 1940, a few days after my eleventh birthday. He served in the British Army during the Sudan Uprising and assassination of General Gordon. He left home when he was fourteen, because he could not get along with his stepmother, and signed on with a oceangoing sailing vessel as a cabin boy. I assume he joined the British Army after his sea adventure. He led a full and fascinating life.

AS I REMEMBER

To me he always seemed tall. He had a hearty laugh, wore bib overalls, a waist-type denim work jacket, and a summer railroad cap. In the winter he wore a heavy cap, which I learned in later life was a Kroemer Cap introduced in the Upper Peninsula for railroad workers. He farmed eighty acres of land four and one-half miles north of Lewiston and was an excellent horseman who took great pride of plowing fields. The furrows that he made were always uniform and straight.   He raised cattle, Durhams I believe, along with Chesapeake hogs and leghorn chickens. He had a dog, Tricksie, and a cat he called Prince Henry.

Prince Henry was a tomcat and had a tendency to leave the farm for nocturnal adventures. Many times he showed up at our farm, and it became the task of the three Gordon and Ruby King kids to take him home. My sisters, Lyllis and Thelma, were two and three years older than me. At any rate, we would gather up Prince Henry in our arms and carry him about a quarter-mile up the hill to Grandpa's house.

He had a well house with a pump jack. The pump jack was powered by a gasoline engine that had huge fly-wheels on each side of the engine. It had a water-cooling tank to keep the engine from over heating, and operated with a flat belt drive to the pump jack. When it was in operation the engine would go putt-putt-putt-putt in rapid succession a few times and not fire again until the momentum from the flywheels had slowed to the point that the governor kicked it in again. The well was 180 feet deep, and the water was pumped to a double-door barn some two hundred feet from the well. The water flowed by gravity to a huge livestock tank that was in the basement of the barn.

The water for household use was carried into the house in a porcelain fourteen-quart pail. If you wanted a drink of water, you used a cup with a long handle with a bend at the end to hang on to the edge of the pail to keep it from sinking to the bottom.

The house was a two-story building that had been moved from Lewiston by teams of horses. This occurred after the sawmill in Lewiston had gone out of business and many of the homes were vacated as working mill families moved away.

I never knew my Grandma King as she had been killed on Halloween night as she walked home from my parents' house along towards dark. A motorist, driving without lights, did not see her walking along the road and hit her. My grandfather later posted a white cross on a fence post along the road. I was born January 21, 1929, so this must have happened October 31, 1928.

Let's get back to Prince Henry. He was a big cat with yellow and white stripes. I guess you would call him a tiger cat. He was a real warrior and had the scars to prove it, though he was never mean to us. I don't ever remember carrying him, as I was the youngest and was considered by my two older sisters as not being qualified to carry him. We would enter the house via the wood shed which always smelled musty. There was about a six-foot boarded section to walk on in the south side of the shed. North of the walkway was the wood piled on a dirt floor. There was a splitting block for splitting kindling. Lots of wood chips were scattered about, and a dull axe with scars on the handle from misguided swings leaned against the chopping block. According to my dad, Grandpa never got the hang of swinging an axe, or sharpening it either.

Jimmy Smith, a cousin, related a story that Grandfather told him about being in the Upper Peninsula. Apparently the snow was deep, because he quoted Grandpa saying in a Scottish brogue, "I chapped, and chapped, and all I chapped was snow."

About fifteen feet from the shed door was the door to the house proper. On the wall left of the opening door was a concave metal mural showing a black gentlemen with whiskers, top hat, toothy smile, and a mule with two jugs of moonshine on the saddle pack. Above all of this was the inscription, "She was bred in old Kentucky." If you looked closely, you could see where Grandpa had scratched on the surface the name of a mare and the date she had been serviced.

The door handle was workable but in the need of service. It dangled down at an obscene angle, but if you lifted up, pushed it in and turned the handle, it would work. The door was not solid. It had two panels of etched glass which you could not see through. We would knock on the door as we had been instructed by our parents. That was a courtesy to be observed even though he was our grandfather.

The dialogue always seemed to be the same regardless of how many times we brought Prince Henry back. One of my sisters would say, "Prince Henry was down at our place, and we brought him back."

"Bully for you," was his reply.

Then he would let out this hearty chuckle and reach down into his bibs and pull out the longest pocket change pouch that I have ever seen. It had two shinny knobs to hold it shut. The pouch was black, but was showing the signs of wear, gray and frayed at the bottom end. He would pour out a handful of change and select three shinny nickels, one for each one of us.

I remember that sometimes there were dishes on the table, apparently left from a previous meal, and saltine crackers, and usually a chunk of cheddar cheese.

Grandfather's kitchen had a large wood-burning cook stove on the north side and a counter on the west wall with a sink for washing dishes and a table for the drinking water pail. There was a fancy cupboard with curved drawers which stored flour and other cooking needs. A pantry door adjoined the kitchen. This room was narrow, with lots of shelves for canned goods, and all kinds of other things. I have no idea what all was in there. I suspect he did not know either.

I forgot to mention, on the way in through the woodshed a four-pane window admitted light into the shed from the south wall. Along that wall in the corner was a five gallon kerosene can. It was not the typical can. This one had a small pump on the top of the can designed for filling kerosene lamps and lanterns. To fill a lamp you held it under a metal spout that swung out from the pump. With the other hand you worked a metal handle up and down to remove the liquid from the five gallon can. It worked very well, eliminating the need for a small funnel and the usual mess that went along with filling lamps. Kerosene was the primary light source for our farm houses and barns.

In the southwest corner of the kitchen was another door which led to the room in which he slept. I don't think it was originally a bedroom and suspect he moved the bed there after the death of my grandmother. It was a double wrought-iron bed, yellow in color. Apparently one of the casters had been lost or broken because a Montgomery Ward catalog held up the left corner.

He had a battery operated Zenith radio that operated on a six-volt storage battery. Twelve-volt batteries did not exist at that time. To improve reception he had an outside aerial going across the roof and attached to I do not know what. This aerial was made of fine twisted copper wire. It ran down from the roof, through the window, wrapped around the bedstead to increase reception, and finally connected to the radio which was on a stand close to his bed. The house had been wired for electricity when it was located in Lewiston, but after it had been moved from town all of the receptacles and switches had been plastered over and repainted.

Lightning and thunderstorms threatened to take his life, and property, many times. It struck one time when he was on one of his horses down by the gate at the entrance to the farm. He was knocked off the horse and rattled a bit, but he survived.

Another time it struck his barn which was loaded with hay in both mows. He had strung more copper wire, this time from the hay track in the peak of the barn. It was a braided copper wire attached to the hay track, run down to the ground some fifty feet below and grounded to a galvanized pipe driven into the ground. The lightning strike apparently entered on the hay track to the copper wire, down the wire a few feet, back into the barn through a pitch fork stuck in the hay, back to the copper wire, down to the ground pipe, and ended up blowing a huge piece of concrete from the north basement wall of the barn. The net result was a few splintered pieces of boards on the barn wall, a splintered pitchfork handle and a hole in the wall of the barn.

We have one more thunderstorm to consider in the life and time of Sylvester King. This time he was in bed with his nightshirt and night cap on. He was sound asleep when it struck. If the clap of thunder did not wake him up, the next sequence of events surely did. The lightning entered the building via the radio aerial from the roof and traveled through the window, through the bed, through the radio, and all through the house where the covered up old wiring went throughout the building.

He woke up with a start. He smelled blown plaster and burning paper. Yep, the catalog had been set on fire. After putting the fire out, he grabbed his .25 caliber automatic pistol which he kept under his pillow at night, ran outside and fired a few shots in the air in a call for help. My folks had been awakened by the same storm, heard the shots and quickly hurried over to see what the problem was.

He was still in his nightclothes when they arrived and was somewhat shaken, talking a mile a minute, but he still had his sense of humor. He said to my parents, "When that happened, I did not know if I was dead or not so I decided to get up and go to the bathroom."

Grandpa's dog, Tricksie, did not leave home as often as did Prince Henry, his cat, but on occasion she did drop by for a visit. My folks had a flock of sheep, so any dog that showed up was not welcome. This was before World War II, and my cousin Jimmy Smith was staying with us, helping with the farm work and earning a few dollars a month for his efforts, plus his room and board. He would soon be drafted into the U. S. Army for a five year period. Jimmy was a hard worker and fun to be around. He loved to hunt, in and out of hunting season, but was not a very good shot.

Tricksie showed up one morning. Jimmy grabbed my .22 caliber rifle and hollered at her to go home, which she started to do on the run. To speed her on her way and to scare her; he fired one shot. Wouldn't you know, he hit her in the hind leg. The wound was not fatal. She let out a "Ki,Yi, Yi" several times, and disappeared through the fence and back home through the clover field. Sylvester blamed Erik Agren for the wound. I think she healed up okay and finally died of natural causes sometime later.

Another time we were coming back from hunting in Jimmy's car when he spotted what he thought was a chicken hawk. He slammed on the brakes, grabbed the gun while the car was still moving, and blazed away. It was not a hawk but one of Agren's homing pigeons. The Good Lord was watching over us that day as Jimmy missed and the pigeon went on its merry way.

We didn't go many places far from home in those days. My dad, Gordon King, was a member of the Montmorency County Road Commission from 1936 through the 40's. The new Mackinc Straits ferry ship, City of Cheboygan, was being christen ed on a hot summer day in July. Dad and his family had received a special invitation from Michigan Governor Van Waggoner to attend. The whole family, plus Sylvester, went to the affair. There is a picture of him and me standing on the main deck side by side. It was the only time I remember of him being in a suit. He was pretty dapper and wore a Stetson hat.

A few times he went with us to Alpena for shopping, for what other reasons I do not know. If you were in Alpena a must stop for him was the Owl Cafe located on Chisholm Street. It was there that I enjoyed one of my first encounters with a store-bought hamburger, courtesy of Grandpa Sylvester.

CANDY

by Sue Gavine Weaver (2009)

"Friends forever," we always promised each other. We would marry brothers and build houses next door to each other. Our children would be friends and we would make them grow up and marry each other. We would go to the same college and always be together. We were best friends.

I can't remember when we first played together. I can't remember my early childhood without being with her. We both lived "downtown Atlanta," me in an apartment on top of Gavine's Restaurant and she on the corner of West and Park Streets. The Briley Township Park was her front yard. We grew up there, from the time we were old enough to play alone and not have someone watch us. Of course everyone watched us; that's the way it was in a small town.

She was Candy Westcott, red, wild curly hair flying about, with the most beautiful freckles I ever saw on anyone all over her face, her arms, her legs; she was as short as I was tall. I was Susie Gavine, tall gangly, buck teeth and a pony tail, but friends we were. We were even blood sisters.

One summer day, we lay under the old big weeping willow tree behind Mowery's house. We had to be careful that old George Cummins didn't see us. He would yell at us and tell us not to pull tree branches off. We were on an old blanket under that tree when we pricked our fingers with needles until they bled, then rubbed them together mixing her blood with mine, and mine with hers and proclaiming from then on that we were blood sisters.

It was quite an exciting day the first time we were allowed to cross the main street and go over to the school swings to play by ourselves. It was a really fun place with swings, a slide and a merry-go-round in front of the school, facing the Congregational Church. We played there for hours, swinging, pushing each other, seeing who could go the highest. She was always braver than I was.

All of Atlanta was our playground, to a point. We always had to watch out for where the big boys were because they ruled the town and didn't want little girls anywhere near where they were. In the mid 50's there was a beach down in the park. It had sand and out farther in the weeds there was an old wooden raft. When the big boys were on it playing king of the raft, we didn't venture out there very often because we invariably got pushed off into those slimy weeds.

All along the river from the park to the dam were big, beautiful weeping willow trees and a trail that ran through them. We spent hours playing in the woods among the trees, making houses and forts and mud pies and playing house like little girls do.

Sometimes when we were really brave we would sneak over to the old water power building. It was forbidden to go in there, but that was what made it such an adventure. We would sneak through the trees and weeds, being sure that snakes didn't drop down on us out of the willow trees. I don't know who told us about snakes that would jump out of trees and crawl down your neck, but they were real to us and we always watched out for 'em. The old water power building was dark and the floor was wet, and the main room was filled with big wheels and old machinery of some kind. We would sneak in there, oh so carefully, and sit on that wet floor with the musty smell and share our dreams.

We also wanted to swim at the dam. It was the ultimate place to swim, with big willows by the water spillway, a long rope with a huge knot hanging from an upper limb. You had to climb the tree, pull up the rope, then crawl down the tree holding onto the rope, and then, oh what fun, pull back and swing out over the water and let go: splash into the cool water. Over and over again. We didn't think we needed anyone to watch us; we thought we were too big for babysitters, but someone was always there to see that we didn't get hurt.

A big summer outing for us was the annual VFW corn roast at Clear Lake. The day park was then on the north side of the lake. There was always a huge metal wash tub filled with block ice and bottles and bottles of ice cold pop. We could stick our arms down in that icy water and pull out as many bottles of pop as we could drink. There was root beer, grape and orange; we could never decide on which kind and probably drank many of each. The men would barbeque and we would eat and swim. We almost always fell asleep on the way home.

One summer Candy was allowed to go on a day trip with our family. It was before the Mackinaw Bridge was built and a great trip was to go up to Mackinaw City, drive your car on a boat and travel across the Straits of Mackinaw to St. Ignace. You parked your car in the bottom of the ferry and went up on top. There was a covered area and the open deck. I remember she and I sitting there in the front of that boat with the water and wind blowing in our faces, holding hands, our hair flying all over the place, two kids having the time of their lives!

Winter was a fun time for us too. Someone always shoveled an ice rink down in the park and it was a great place to skate, and so convenient; we just put on our skates at Candy's house and ran, or slipped, across the road and out onto the ice. There we would skate until we couldn't feel our feet anymore, take off our skates and run up to the restaurant where my mother, known around town as Mother Gavine, would fix us hot chocolate, the best we ever had. Sometimes she would even make us Boston Coffee, which was a quarter cup coffee, three-quarters cup milk and lots of sugar - mmm...mmm.

Then came the winter of 1957. We always walked to school together, meeting up at the corner of West Street and M-32, crossing the street together talking about whatever little girls talk about. This day, she was carrying her saxophone and I my clarinet. Two friends, together forever, but that was not to be. That day as we played on the back hill during recess, she slid down the hill and someone else came down behind her and they both fell to the ground. She hit her head on the icy hill. She died that night.

The next day was probably the worse day of my ten-year old life. I remember going over to her house. Her mom, Virginia, held me on her lap. She gave me Candy's music box. We lifted the top off of it and it played the music so sweetly as we sat there, Virginia's tears flowing down her face onto mine, mixing with my tears and falling on the music box. My friend was gone forever. I still have that music box and whenever I open it and hear it play I see my friend, her wild red hair, and the memories come rushing back.

The Atlanta Elementary School has ever since had a Jim Foote painted portroit of a red haired, freckled face girl prominently hanging on the wall. It is Candy, my friend.

THE FIRE

By Sue Gavine Weaver (2010)

I drive down the main street of Atlanta and look up at the tall building, closed up and empty with a fairly new facade front and a sign calling it DJ's. The memories of living and growing up in this building come rushing back, especially the night of the fire. It was originally Gavine's Café (later Gavine's Restaurant) downstairs, and for much of my life the upstairs was my home.

When my mother and dad came to Atlanta in 1946 to build their restaurant, Gavine's Café, they came at the urging of their good friends, Russell and Ella Benson. They had already built a bar next door to an empty lot, ideal for a restaurant. After much discussion and planning, my dad and Russell decided (wisely?) that it would be more economical to attach the restaurant to the bar with one common wall. It was not an idea that my mother was in favor of. Later, her reluctance was proven to have been well founded.

Gavine's Café was built next to Benson's Bar and the two businesses served the people of Atlanta. An apartment was built on top of the restaurant for us, the Gavine family, to live in. This was the home that I grew up in and loved. In the winter of 1952, my mother's worst fears were realized.

It was late at night, my sister Nancy babysitting for the Englehart children, sister Sally asleep in her bedroom in the front, my parents sleeping in the back bedroom. I was on a roll-away in their room.

Jim "Father" Gavine in front of Gavine's Café during the early 1950's

I remember waking up and calling out to them, "Mama, daddy, I smell gas."

It took several calls for me to wake them up; the smell of what I thought was gas was stifling. My mother jumped out of bed and looked out the back window. She couldn't see anything at all, just smoke billowing up everywhere. She opened the window, smoke rolled in, she slammed it shut. All she could see was smoke, smoke in the sky and all around the back yard.

"Jim! Jim!," she called. "The restaurant is on fire!"

There was great confusion! Mother was screaming at Nancy and Sally, "Girls, get up! get up! get dressed!" In her excitement she had forgotten that Nancy wasn't there. My heart was pounding, I was crying as I hurried to dress.

"Put on warm clothes, hurry! hurry," she directed.

I remember we were running through the house, the four of us, running, running, down the stairs, into the dark, out to the street! By this time someone had called in the fire and the town fire siren was screaming in the night air. The volunteer fire fighters were on the way. It didn't take them long to see that this would be a big one.

Smoke! Smoke! everywhere! "Where's Nancy? Where's Nancy?" My mother was looking for her missing daughter. Sally, crying, finally remembered that Nancy was babysitting and was safe.

People were all over the streets, many yelling, "Get back! Get back!" Fire was shooting in the air. The air was hot from the fire. Water hoses were pouring water up and onto the buildings, smoke and steam rolling up into the dark night sky. Fire departments from neighboring towns where called to help. The fire truck ran out of water so they attached the hoses together and ran them from the river up to the bar.

"Save the restaurant! Save the restaurant!" someone yelled. Benson's Bar was burning down.

As we stood on the street shivering in the cold watching the bar and our restaurant burn, Jean and Glen Erity came across the street from their Sport Shop carrying boots, scarfs and mittens for us to wear.

The next thing I remember was waking up in a bed over at the Benson's house. We were all there, the Bensons, Mom, Dad, Nancy, Sally and me. We were safe. Everyone was talking about the fire.

We had only the clothes we had worn when we ran out. I could still smell the smoke that clung to us. We lived with the Bensons until the restaurant could be cleaned and repaired. The whole inside was smoke filled and the walls were black from the smoke. Benson's Bar was gone.

My mother and dad went to the restaurant and got some of our clothes. She and Ella washed them the best they could. But the smell of smoke lingered everywhere, in the clothes, in the restaurant, in the apartment. We could smell smoke for a long time afterwards.

After the fire there was nothing left of the bar except a pile of bricks and twisted metal and about a quarter of the restaurant wall was gone. When spring came, the townspeople got together to help clean up the rubble and brick up the gapping hole in the restaurant wall. Soon, a new Benson's Bar was built.

We moved back to our home above the restaurant. I grew up there, many times hearing my mother remind my dad that if a double wall had been built the damage to the restaurant wouldn't have been so bad. We talked about it often and I have never forgotten our close call the night of the fire.

A GHOST TOWN

By Craig Sherwood (1932)

Last summer, Bob and I went on a week's camping trip. On the way back we came upon on an old smoke trail through the country and it was a hot day. Each step we took, little clouds of dust rose up. Our packs were heavy and I was really thirsty. We had walked about two hours and we were just hiking along, rather mechanically, hoping that over the next hill we would see the old cinder bed. We knew that when we reached it we would find plenty of shade and a drink of cold water from a spring.

At last we came over the brow of a hill and below us was a wide valley. At the top of the hill was a narrow plain which sloped down to the edge of the swamp. The road went down the hill and turned to the right, worming along the edge of the swamp. Directly in front of us and extending to the right along the swamp were several branched trails on woods of cinder. We had come to the old cinder bed.

We went down to the edge of the swamp, located the spring, and washed and got dinner. After we had eaten we went out under a wild apple tree and lay down on the grass. Back on the hill we had come down there was an old log cabin hidden by the brush. As I looked at it I seemed to drift back to the old logging days when the now so called old cinder bed was a flowering timber town called Valentine. It was a headquarters of the D. & M. Railroad, which explained the long branching beds of fine black cinders. The railroad company had their engine shop there and they used to clean out the flues and fire box of the engines which explains long beds of fine black cinder. In my mind's eye, I could see the long main street running parallel and on the opposite side of the railroad with its row of buildings on the far side at the foot of the hill.

At one side of the street was a blacksmith's shop with two teams tied to the rail before the wide, open-fronted structure. From within came the clang of the anvil. Next there was an old shed that was used as a general catch-all. The next building in line was the general store and post office. It had a high false front and a roof that extended from the front of the building out over the board walk, forming a sort of canopy. Under this were several men sitting on boxes and kegs talking over the hard times. The next building of importance was the town's one and only hotel. It had a wide porch and a veranda on which perched benches, the same as the general store. The place had a more lively air about it for there was a bar in connection with the establishment. The strains of sweet music came drifting across the street.

Going on down the board walk I saw two more stores and a saloon. At the far end of the street was an old dilapidated horse stable.

In back of these places of business were the dwelling houses. Most of the housing was on the hill; the most prominent one was the log cabin owned by old Doc Valentine. It was after this old settler that the village was named.

Over the whole place there was a feeling of laziness broken only by the occasional tromping of booted feet on the board walk or the lugging of an engine. But on Saturday you would see a great transformation. The lumber jacks and their families would be in and everything would be alive with people and voices. The street would be lined with wagons and buggies.

Just then, Bob gave me a poke and said that we had better be hitting the trail. With a sigh I brought my thoughts back to the present and looked at old Doc Valentine's cabin perched on the hill and the old railroad bed covered with cinders. These were the only things left to mark the location of the town.

We shouldered out packs and turned out backs on one of Michigan's ghost towns.

Notes:

Claudia Sherwood submitted this story which was written by her father for an English class while he was a student at Michigan State College in 1932. It features the old town site of Valentine, one of the county's early logging com-

munities, which was also the location of a Detroit and Mackinaw Railroad engine shop. For that reason it was known as the cinder bed for years after the town and the railroad branch were deserted. Valentine was located north of Atlanta near the intersection of M-33 and Rush Lake Road.

    The late Craig Sherwood was the son of Claude and Evelyn Sherwood. Claude was an Atlanta businessman and served as the school board president for many years. In fact, he handed my diploma to me in 1961. Evelyn was the sister of Harrison Baker and was active in many local church and community activities.

    Claudia did not know who "Bob" was, but thought he might have been Bob Stevens, my father's first cousin, who was a contemporary with Craig in high school. – Dan Stevens

PART III

"He was born in (Motmorency County) Michigan in 1905, the son of a farmer and lumberman. He died in Michigan in 1967, a farmer and lumberman... In between, he changed conservation in North Carolina forever." Such were the words written and spoken about Ross O. Stevens, my father, at his posthumous induction into the North Carolina Conservation Hall of Fame on February 9, 2001.

Indeed, Dad had been a leader in bringing professional and scientific conservation methods to North Carolina. He spent twenty years in the state, first as the regional wildlife manager for the U.S. Soil Conservation Service, then as the head of the wildlife management program at North Carolina State University and textbook author, and finally, as Executive Director of the North Carolina Wildlife Federation.

However, his true love was Montmorency County, Michigan, to which he eagerly returned in 1952, twenty-seven years after being a member of Atlanta High School's first graduating class and twenty-one years after earning his second degree at the University of Michigan School of Forestry. That he truly loved northern Michigan was firmly implanted in my mind during my early years in North Carolina through nightly bedtime stories about his experiences as a boy in Kellyville, at his dad's lumber camp, and with his horse, Bucko.

Here, he was a happy man as he raised Hereford cattle on his farm in Pleasant Valley, operated a small timbering and sawmill operation, and participated fully in Montmorency County activities. He helped organize an Atlanta area sportsman's club, was the Briley Township Supervisor, a member of the Montmorency County Board of Supervisors, and served three terms in the Michigan House of Representatives.

During the last two years of his life, in failing health, he penned seven stories about early Montmorency County which were published in the Montmorency County Tribune in 1966-67. The stories are included here.

Dan Stevens

HUNGER IN THE WILDERNESS OF EARLY MONTMORENCY COUNTY

by Ross O. Stevens (1966)

Our story involves two families who were among the earliest settlers in Montmorency County. Mostly the story comes from Henry Meyers, a son of one of the families, who will be eighty years old on February 21, 1967. It all happened many years before Henry was born. His father died when Henry was six years old, but his mother told and retold the story many times.

The two families were the Charles Meyers family from Oldenburg, Germany, and the August Bargehr family from Austria. The Meyers family had homesteaded land near the north side of Spiess Lake five miles west of Atlanta, where Henry Meyers now lives. The Bargehr homestead included Spiess Lake and adjoining land on the south side of present Highway M-32. Spiess Lake first was known as Bargehr Lake and later as Remington Lake. (Since this story was written, a developer renamed it Lake Inez) The creek leading from the lake still is called Barger Creek, although with the new spelling.

The year was about 1875. The closest source of groceries and supplies was Otsego Lake about twenty-four miles as the crow flies and probably closer to thirty miles as these early settlers had to travel to miss lakes, swamps, and rugged hills.

Charles Meyers and August Bargehr had become good friends while attending college together in the Old Country. Apparently both were from prominent and well-to-do families. Charles Meyers had inherited a shoe factory, but Germany was at war with France and Charles had to serve in the army. His military service ended in 1871. Due to many unfavorable circumstances he sold his factory, salvaged a small sum of money and made plans to go to America with his wife Louise and two children, Hanse and Gertie.

In the meantime August Bargehr had married an opera singer. Because female entertainers were looked upon with disfavor at that time in Austria, August was disinherited by his family.

Discouraged and practically penniless, August Bargehr wrote to his friend Charles Meyers in Germany. When he learned of Charles' plans to go to America, August decided that he, too, would take his wife and baby daughter to America, the land he had heard was full of opportunity and freedom.

Shortly the two young families were on their way to American and wilderness homes. After paying their boat fares they had very little money.

How these families reached Detroit from New York is an unknown part of our story, but they arrived there probably in early summer of 1874. The women and children were left in Detroit while the men worked their way to Alpena on a boat. They went to Alpena because a government land office was located there and they could choose homestead sites.

With a government "land looker" as a guide, they set out to find their future homes. They walked all the way from Alpena and back again, more than ninety miles round trip. There were no roads, no paths, nor any markers over much of the way.

The men returned to Detroit. They and their families then traveled to Otsego Lake by train. There they hired an ox team and wagon to take them, their scant belongings and some supplies to their new homes in the dense wilderness.

A trail road led eastward from Otsego Lake. It was just wide enough for a wagon to wind among the pine trees. It finally ended in hardwood country at the homestead of the Proctor family on what is now the Lewiston road about three miles south of the M-32 junction, where now stands a stone house on the east side of the road.

Because it was late in the fall and because the road ended there, the Bargehr and Meyers families set up their tents at the Proctor place and prepared to spend the winter.

Not being used to hard physical work and especially not being used to working with axes and crosscut saws, Charles and August spent nearly a year making an ox cart path to their new homes near Spiess Lake. Later this path was known as the Old German Road because so many German families traveled over it to settle in this area. Parts of the road still are visible.

September 1875 found the Bargehrs and Meyers and their children living in tents near a spring of clear, cold water at the foot of the hill just south of the present buildings on the Meyers farm. A trail road led to the closest neighbor some ten miles away; a dense hardwood forest stood all around. It was too late in the season to build even a small house because it would have to be built of logs and poles. It would be impossible to haul enough lumber with oxen all the way from Otsego Lake.

There was no land cleared, no crops to harvest, so the men spent their time catching fish, killing wild game, learning the country and gathering wild foods. They did not fare too badly until a blizzard ushered in an early winter. Through the years, old timers repeated the story of the near tragedy that befell the Meyers and Bargehr families that first winter on their new homestead.

Having no horses or other beasts of burden during the first year or two, Charles Meyers and August Bargehr had to carry food and necessary supplies over a trail marked by blazed trees from Otsego Lake. It was a long hike at best, and they made the journey only when absolutely necessary for food or other supplies.

Apparently the fall and winter of 1875 was unusual. Rainy, snowy weather cut down on the men's activities. During good weather they tried to kill game for food, but game was relatively scarce. The fact that they were inexperienced woodsmen did not help matters.

Despite efforts to stockpile food, the supply dwindled. Finally the long trip to Otsego Lake was decided upon as the surest and quickest way to provide food for those hungry children and grown folk.

On the morning the men were to start the long journey a raging snowstorm was in progress. They decided to wait; tomorrow would be a better day, they hoped. But it wasn't. Snow was falling rapidly, and on the third day it was more of the same.

On the morning of the fourth day there was no choice, they had to start out. More than two feet of new snow covered the ground. The food supply had dwindled to only one loaf of bread and a few scraps. The men insisted on leaving the bread for the women and children. However, the women talked it over and decided there would be no chance of the men getting to Otsego Lake without food. The women tricked them into thinking there were two loaves of bread instead of one.

With one loaf of bread and a handful of matches, the men headed westward along the tree-blazed trail. The going was slow and very tiring. When darkness prevented them from   following the tree blazes any longer, they built a fire and huddled around it until dawn. At the break of day they trudged on. Finally they reached the Otsego Lake railroad where there was a lumber camp and a store. After eating a hearty meal at the lumber camp, the very tired men bought as much food as they could carry and headed eastward toward home, constantly anxious about their families.

By this time the snow was waist deep in many places. Their heavy packs made walking even more difficult.

In the meantime, the women and children in their tent at the foot of the hill near the little lake had cooked and eaten every last crumb and every last scrap they could find. They had wood to keep the fire burning in the little tin stove, but no food. The children were crying from sheer hunger.

The possibility of starving to death was so real that Mrs. Bargehr approached Mrs. Meyers with the idea of killing the children and then drawing straws to determine which one of them would be the last to die at her own hand.

Mrs. Meyers would not listen to this idea. What an awful thing it would be for the men to return and find them all dead, was her reasoning. Instead they agreed to renew their efforts to find some little morsel of food. Perhaps they could shoot a red squirrel or a blue jay. Perhaps they could find a chipmunk hibernating under the snow covered tree trunks the men had stacked just outside the tent as a fuel supply.

Dressed as warmly as possible, the women started searching for something that would cheat death a day or two longer. One by one they lifted the old tree trunks from the snow and watched eagerly for some sign of life under each. Almost the entire pile had been searched when between two logs that lay on the ground a mouse's nest was spotted. Almost at the same time the women fell to their knees and covered the nest tightly with their hands, but if any mouse had been there, it had been forewarned by the disturbance.

To their surprise and joy, however, the women found that the mice had stored food in the nest, most of it being rice the little creatures had pilfered from the nearby tent in better days.

Every seed, every kernel of rice, about a half cup full in all, was carefully removed from the nest, washed and made into soup for the children. Starvation was held at bay.

It is not certain whether this all happened on the fourth, fifth or sixth day after the men departed for Otsego Lake, but it is known that when the snowstorm subsided, bitter cold set in.

Within a few miles of their journey's end, darkness overtook the weary travelers, but they were determined to reach home that night. When they could see or feel the blazed trees no longer, they tried to follow a course that would take them home but soon realized that they were completely lost. They concluded that home must be within a mile or two, but in what direction they did not know. Slowly they trudged to the top of a steep hill, removed their heavy packs and decided to rest a short while.

The women back at the tents had become very apprehensive because the men had not returned. They were desperately hungry; they were just about ready to give up. The evening before they had fired several rifle shots into the air, just in case the men were near enough to hear. They decided to do the same again.

Sure enough, the first shot brought a faint reply. Every little while after that the men would call loudly and the women would answer with a rifle shot.

However, the story is not finished. At the west end of Spiess Lake were several springs which had become covered with snow and had not frozen. In making a bee-line to the rifle signals, Meyers fell into a spring almost to his waist. Bargehr pulled him out. Then, though they were now less than a quarter of a mile away from home, by the time the men reached their tents the unfortunate Mr. Meyers' clothing and boot on one side were frozen stiff as a board, and one foot was frozen.

The boot on the frozen foot had to be cut away with a sharp knife. After the children were fed and tucked into bed, the adults spent several hours restoring near normal circulation to the frosted foot and leg.

Never again did they allow the cupboards to become so bare.

POSTSCRIPT: Many other events occurred during the early days to these settlers when Montmorency County was still a part of Alpena County.

Within a few years many more homesteaders had settled in the Big Rock-Kellyville areas as well as other parts of what would become Montmorency County. By 1880 the Meyers and Bargehrs had cleared several acres and several neighbors were within a few miles. These two pioneer families hosted many of these neighbors when they came to locate their new homesteads.

The Indians who hunted and fished this wilderness before white settlers took over likewise liked to stop at the Meyers' and Bargehr's places. In return for the hospitality the Indians would give beaver carcasses for food. Beaver tails were especially welcome since the fat could be burned for light and for cooking.

Interestingly enough, the Spiess Lake area had been chosen by Meyers and Bargehr because on the little creek a short distance below the lake was a site suitable for a dam and a grist mill such as was common in their homelands of Germany and Austria. A dam was partly constructed and its remains still are visible. The project was never completed.

Before many years passed tragedy struck the Bargehr family. Mrs. Bargehr gave birth to twins but in the ordeal lost her own life. Already Briley Cemetery, west of Atlanta, had been established, and Mrs. Bargehr's is one of the unmarked graves there.

Shortly after his wife died, the heart-broken August Bargehr and his three children returned to his native land. The twins were stricken with illness and died on the boat to Austria.

The Meyers family stayed on in the Big Rock area a few years and then moved to the rapidly developing Hillman area from where Charles served as a county official. Henry was born in Hillman, February 21, 1887. His father died six years later. The old homestead near Spiess Lake still remains in the Meyers family. Henry's brother, Hans, raised a large family there.

THE MYSTERIOUS BABY AWAKENER IN EARLY MONTMORENCY COUNTY

By Ross O. Stevens (1966)

My father, George Stevens, and my mother, Gertie Stevens, came to Montmorency County to live in 1897. My oldest brother, Harold (Bud), was two years old. My mother left behind her parents and a large family of sisters and brothers from near St. Johns, Michigan, and like many other young mothers, had a longing to return home after a few years to see her relatives and friends.

My folks had come to these parts from southern Michigan in a wagon pulled by a pair of mules. They slept under the wagon at night, with a piece of canvas thrown over the top of it to protect them from rain if it should come. Many times my father told how their food and money became exhausted except for a jar of sour milk. At meal time he would stop at a farm house or lumber camp and offer to trade the sour milk for food. Always he received food but no one wanted the milk. They traveled nearly a hundred miles bartering the sour milk for food.

While the mules brought them here without too much discomfort, it was not worth it to use this method to return home for a visit. The only other way to go south in those early days was to be taken to the thriving little town of Valentine that was located near the present-day junction of the Rush Lake Road and M-33 and from there ride the Detroit and Mackinaw train to Alpena and then southward.

It was in 1901 that my mother set forth on this venture to her homeland. My father took her to Valentine with a horse and buggy. There was to be a square dance at the hotel in Valentine that night so my folks planned to attend the dance, and my mother could board the train the next day. They stabled the horse in the livery barn and checked in at the hotel. In addition to the older brother Bud, my brother Grove had come along and was about a year old. He presented the problem.

By the time the dance started Grove had been tucked safely in bed and was fast asleep. The folks put out the light and proceeded to the dance floor just one flight of stairs down. In just a few minutes one of the hotel helpers reported to my mother that the baby was crying. She hurried up the stairway and sure enough Grove was exercising his lungs in good shape. Mother struck a match and lit the kerosene lamp on the little table on one side of the room and proceeded to comfort the child. In a few minutes Grove was sound asleep again. Perhaps a little colic pain, my mother thought as she rejoined my father at the dance.

Lo and behold, in just a little while the baby was crying at the top of his lungs. Again my mother went to the room, lit the light and could find nothing wrong with the baby, except that he seemed to want to go to sleep. He was sleeping soundly in just a few minutes. Again the light was blown out and the downward flight of steps pursued.

Another little while and Grove was bellowing so loudly that the rafters of that old wooden hotel virtually were shaking. Both Mother and Dad trekked upstairs that time, my dad a little bit irritated, allowing that he would find out what was ailing with that youngster. Dad lit the lamp.

Mother went straight to the bed, "Oh," she screamed as a dozen or so little creatures scampered from Grove's face and arms as the room lit up. "Bed bugs," she exclaimed.

They looked under the pillow and cover and sure enough bed bugs were in every hiding place available. As soon as the lights were blown out, these little animals would come forth and soon were trying to satisfy their appetites at the expense of baby Grove. The whole problem was solved simply by leaving the little old kerosene light burning. Bed bugs are repulsed by light.

This little story is true, but it only hints at a serious problem of the early settlers. The bed bug was just one of several insect pests that made life more difficult. Many modern chemicals were not even dreamed of that presently help keep such things subdued.

Probably not a single lumbering camp existed in those days which was not loaded with bed bugs. They would hide in crevices, in bedsteads and other furniture, and in clothing, and in fact, in any place they could find darkness. Not until darkness came and the lights were blown out, would they begin the evening meal hunt.

Nearly always some children from lumbering camp settlements attended the little one-room country schools of those days, and therefore these institutions of learning in many instances became places of insect exchange. Desks, benches and chairs that the children sat on were good hiding places, and it was a lucky family indeed, that did not have at least one encounter with these little pests.

How many children today even know what bed bugs look like? It's just as well that they don't!

Oddly enough these creatures took advantage of another night feeding animal, the bat, to gain their worldly ends. Out at night bed bugs would crawl on a bat and eat their dinner in transit as the bat flew from one attic or woodshed or such to another. When his host alighted the bug would crawl away to a new home, perhaps lay eggs and start a whole new generation. It made no difference to them whether the family was rich or poor. Especially did bud bed bugs seem to congregate under the bark of dead hemlock trees and old logs. In those days nearly every family had a woodshed for fuel storage, and many times both bats and bed bugs frequented these.

As late as when I started at the Kellyville School in 1911 or 1912, bed bugs were a major concern. I can remember my mother putting us through the wringer, so to speak, many times in her fight to keep us free of these embarrassing creatures.

Lice that thrived on humans in those old days were about in the same class as bed bugs. Here again schools were a prime spreading agency. More than once my mother made us wash our heads in kerosene because she had found a louse on one of us. Then after a certain number of days, the process was repeated to destroy any babies that might have hatched from eggs. The kerosene treatment was just about universal in those days. Oh, how I hated it!

HOLDING THE TRAIN HOSTAGE FOR JUSTICE IN EARLY MONTMORENCY COUNTY

By Ross O. Stevens (1966)

In general the people who came to settle the north were honest, hard working and very neighborly. A few were different. All wanted to better themselves. Sometimes drastic measures were used to deter individuals who would take advantage of others.

One incident involved my father, George Stevens. I remember it well because as an eleven-year old boy, I was left to watch our old team of horses hitched to the railroad track while my father put some finishing touches to some touchy business.

During the years when my father worked as a laborer at one dollar per day, then as a foreman at Kelly's mill in Kellyville, and later as a jobber for Kneeland-Biglow Company, he managed to save a few dollars. With his savings bought a few forty-acre blocks of timberland mostly for $20.00 per forty with the hope of starting a lumbering operation of his own some day.

His opportunity came shortly after the Boyne City, Gaylord and Alpena Railroad became a reality. One forty acres of swamp timber owned by my father was just a stone's throw from the Green Branch of the B.C.G.& A. which extended from near Green's crossing eastward and northward to the then deserted town of Valentine. Earlier the Detroit and

Mackinac Railway had extended a branch southward and then westward from Valentine. When the B.C.G.& A. came through it used much of the same roadbed for its extension to Valentine. Now M-33 follows these same old routes for several miles. The particular forty acres that my father owned was just west and north of where the Rouse Road now intersects with M-33.

The years between 1915 and 1918 were when my father ventured forth on his own with very little except good credit and a will to work. Somehow he set up a small camp cook shack and bunkhouse combined with a horse barn that would accommodate about four teams. Another little building served as the office and bunkhouse for my dad. Attached to it was a sort of lean-to that housed our own team of horses. The main parts of the buildings were made of logs and a clay-mortar chinking between the logs.

In those days the custom was for small jobbers to cut timber and haul it to a banking ground on the railroad and then sell it the following spring. The lumberjacks and my father worked hard that winter and by spring had many long rows of eight-foot pulpwood, cedar ties and fence posts stacked beside the railroad track in the vicinity of where Rouse Road meets M-33. Naturally my father was anxious to sell. He had borrowed money to pay the men and to buy supplies.

Farther north a second party was banking timber on the Green Branch, and because it was a big customer of the railroad, had the idea that the timber banked along this branch must be sold to them. At first there was no problem. The boss of the outfit looked at the Stevens' timber and made an offer to buy. No harm in that but after several more visits which ended with this other party almost insisting that Dad sell to them the situation became aggravating.

Within a few weeks Dad sold his timber to other buyers who wanted it loaded out as fast as possible. Several times railroad cars were ordered, but each time the railroad crew made excuses for failure to comply. Soon it became obvious that the party who first wanted to buy the timber was influencing the railroad employees. This party thought that if they could stall long enough my father would be forced to sell to them.

In the meantime Dad learned of another forty acres for sale, and when he checked it he found that the railroad crossed one corner of it. Dad bought the forty acres for $150, had the title checked and found that the B.C.G.&A. railroad had not obtained the right to cross this particular land.

Soon boxcars were again ordered, and this time when the train pulled north on the Green Branch Dad was ready. After the train passed over the little corner of the recently purchased Stevens property, Dad hitched his team to one rail and waited.

Shortly the train reappeared. The three cars that Dad had ordered were attached to the rear. As the train approached Dad proceeded to flag it down. At first it appeared the train would not stop and Dad was about ready to give the horses the word to pull.

After a lot of heated words on both sides, Dad showed the train crew the corner to his property and explained how the railroad company was trespassing. There was no doubt that the rails would have been pulled far enough apart to derail the engine had there been any effort to proceed further with the train.

Realizing this fact, the train crew invited Dad aboard and reversed itself to the piled timber. I was left holding the team's reigns with instructions to keep hooked to the rail until the cars were delivered and uncoupled from the train.

From then until the B.C.G.& A. ended its operations in our county, Dad shipped hundreds of carloads of timber and never again did he have trouble getting railcars when and where he wanted them.

TRAVELING IN EARLY MONTMORENCY COUNTY

By Ross O. Stevens (1966)

Railroad and horses played important parts in Montmorency County's early history. Much could be told about a man's character in the early days by the horses he owned and the way he treated them. Horses were a main source of power.

Four different railroads operated within the county at one time or another. All were gone by 1935. Probably the earliest railroad was the narrow gauge that entered from Comins way. The D. and M. from Alpena through Hillman and the Lewiston branch of the Michigan Central each played important parts. It would be interesting to prepare a map* showing all branches of these roads and a story of their main purposes.

The Boyne City, Gaylord and Alpena Railroad came and went entirely within my memory. It is involved in this story as related mostly by Harrison Baker, who until recently had a dairy farm a few miles southwest of Atlanta.

In 1922 Harrison Baker was just becoming established in these parts. In late March of that year a tremendous snowstorm added to an already heavy layer of snow. Heavy winds caused much drifting. If Harrison had known what trouble he was heading for when he boarded the train in Atlanta on his way to Gaylord and thence to Detroit, he probably would have stayed home.

The plan was to catch the noon southbound train at Gaylord, but a few miles east of Gaylord the B.C.G. and A. train was stopped by a high snow drift and did not reach Gaylord until about four that afternoon. Supposing the noon train had long since departed, Harrison started looking for a place to eat.

Shortly a train whistle blew, and looking westward on Gaylord's main street, Harrison saw a southbound passenger train about to stop. He rushed to the depot to find that this was the morning train just getting in. It, too, had been stuck in drifted snow.

Harrison boarded the train and was much happier when it headed southward. His happiness did not last long. Several miles south of Gaylord the train plowed into a king-sized snowbank where the road bed had been cut through a hill. There is was stuck.

Hours later the noon train pulled up behind. Instead of passengers it carried a large crew of laborers who proceeded to remove the mountain of snow with wheelbarrows and shovels. In the meantime a snowplow came to help from the south, but one push into the huge drift was enough for it. It was lucky to be able to back up.

It was way after midnight before a path was finished and wheels started turning again. Luckily, the train carried a dining car and all passengers were served coffee and donuts. For Harrison, it was two donuts and a cup of coffee from breakfast to breakfast.

Harrison's main purpose in going to Detroit was to get the money to pay for the newly acquired Baker property, but other things required Mr. Baker to be gone about ten days. Several days before he returned to these parts the weather turned extremely warm and it seemed like all the thick layers of snow wanted to melt and get out of the country all at once.

When Harrison stepped from the train in Gaylord on his way back, the town was full of lumberjacks, most likely because of the sudden spring break-up and the irregular train schedule. The train to Atlanta had not run for several days because of washouts in the road bed.

"I was scared," Harrison related. "There I was with all that money and those big bruising lumberjacks all around me and no way to get to Atlanta. I didn't know what to do."

But he did do something. He went into the men's room, locked the door, put the money which was in large bills in an envelope and put it in the bottom of his arctic covered shoe. In this way he thought his money at least could not be taken without him knowing it. If he had to stay overnight he would sleep with his shoes on.

Once again out in the depot waiting room, a voice called, "Hello, Harrison, what are you doing here?" He turned and there was Grove Rouse who had just gotten off the same train.

Harrison pulled Rouse to one side and told him he had a lot of money with him and he was uneasy about it with all those people around.

"Well," said Grove, who knew lumberjacks from way back and who had much to do with early Montmorency County history, "I have a lot of money, too, but I'd a thousand times rather be here among these lumberjacks than on the streets of Detroit. But," he added, "we are not going to stay here overnight. I think I know how we can get to Atlanta yet this afternoon if I can find a telephone." At that time automobiles did not travel during the winter months.

About an hour later a Model T Ford sedan with railroad car wheels stopped in front of the Gaylord depot. Mr. Rouse motioned to Harrison and soon they were passengers on the B.C.G. and A. line headed for Atlanta. Mr. Rouse had called the railroad headquarters in Boyne City and the road master, a Mr. White, had brought this remodeled rail car.

All went well for the three men in the rail car until they approached the East Branch of the Black River. Here, the whole area looked more like a lake than a railroad track crossing a river. Water was everywhere and for a long way no part of the railroad track was visible. Mr. White said he had been over that part of the track the day before and assured his passengers all would be well.

But this day the water was a little higher and somewhere along the East Branch the high water had loosened a part of a large cedar tree trunk. A branch or knot or something had caught on the rail and there it was blocking the way. Mr. White bumped it gently with the front wheel, but it was evident that to push it more would only cause the back part to swing around and hit the rail car which could have caused a worse situation.

After backing the car several feet the men paused to study their predicament. To back all the way to Gaylord or even far enough to reach help was out of the question.

"What do you know," began Mr. White, "we haven't even a bottle to keep us company."

With just a little help that log would go on down the river they all agreed. But who would want to wade in that cold water?

"Tell you what we'll do, suggested Mr. Rouse. "I have a deck of cards. We'll play two games of rum. The loser will get out and move the log. No use of all of us getting wet." Mr. White agreed with this plan.

Mr. Baker was not much of a card player and he had other problems. What if he lost? The water would certainly go over the top of his arctic boots and the money in his shoe would become wet and probably badly dilapidated. If he removed his arctics and shoes he surely would expose the place he hid his money and this would be embarrassing.

Mr. Rouse, who knew his way around with cards won the first game. Mr. White and Mr. Baker started the second, but Mr. Baker just could not concentrate on his card game. All he could think about was what he would do if he lost.

Mr. White was out to win and it looked as though he would do it easily.

"Hey, isn't that our log going down the river?" asked Mr. Rouse. Quickly they looked to the front and sure enough, the way was clear.

"Jumping Jupiter!" exclaimed Mr. Baker. "You're the luckiest man on this trip," quipped Mr. Rouse.

"I never want to make another like it," Mr. Baker concluded.

Mr. White was busy starting the motor. After several sputters and chugs and much water kicking out of the exhaust pipe, the contraption started to ease forward. Within a half hour, all were in Atlanta.

ROSS STEVENS NOTE: Well do I remember the 1922 floods. At that time I was riding my pony, Buckoo, from Kellyville to Atlanta High School each day. When we arrived at Hay Meadow Creek north of the present Boyne Products factory, the bridge was gone completely. We backtracked to Melrose's crossing and followed the B.C.G. and A. railroad tracks to the depot. Several other bridges had also washed out.

Just south of the town hall Mr. Newland owned a large shephard dog which came bounding out at the cantering Buckoo. The crazy house jumped sideways and took off at full speed. In attempting to pull him up I broke the left rein.

Right then I knew trouble was coming. The pony would turn west on the main street. The corner was completely covered with rough ice packed by the sleighs and horses during the winter just ending. Buckoo went down and we both went skidding across the street. Somehow my feet remained free, and when the horse stopped skidding I stepped off his back. No damage except a few bruises.

* *Several years after Ross died in June, 1967, his brother, Arno (Doc) Stevens, researched and published a map showing the location of the railroads which had operated in Montmorency County.*

WAYLAID ONCE TOO OFTEN IN EARLY MONTMORENCY COUNTY

By Ross O. Stevens (1967)

"I didn't take a chance on being waylaid the fourth time", explained the late Eugene La Pointe as he tapped the ashes from his pipe in the living room of his Atlanta home on Airport Road.

Gene, as he was known to his multitude of friends, had long since retired and was not able to get about too well. He called me to his home to discuss business. When that was finished, we talked about early pine lumbering days in Montmorency County.

Mr. La Pointe, a husky lad, originally lived in Alpena. In his middle teens he started working as a lumberjack. Soon he learned to handle the cross-cut saw and the axe with the best. His bosses knew he was a good man to have in a lumber camp.

When he was about 20 years old, he worked in a large lumber camp in the vicinity of Rainey Lake north of Atlanta. Pay was about seventy-five cents to one dollar a day plus board and a bunk to sleep in. Working hours were long. The camp Gene worked at was located near a branch of the Detroit and Mackinaw railroad that extended from Alpena to Hillman and thence to many parts of northern Montmorencey County.

This particular branch passed through Valentine, a prosperous little lumber town located mostly on the west side of the present M-33, about a half mile north of the Rush Lake Road. A postoffice was located there along with a rather large hotel, a liquor saloon, a school, stores, and several houses.

Valentine was a railroad hub. Three branches led out from there. One extended generally southward, a second generally westward, and a third northward to the Clear Lake, Tomahawk Lake, Rainey Lake areas.

Young Mr. La Pointe had been at the Rainey Lake camp several months when he decided to go home to see his parents. He had accumulated what was then a fairly good stake, perhaps a hundred dollars.

The train generally carried one passenger car, but its main activity was hauling log cars to the huge saw mills in Alpena.

Gene boarded the train at his camp, and soon was in Valentine. There the other passengers and he left the train while it proceeded to pick up the rest of its load from points along the other branches that extended out from Valentine. Sometimes this process would require three or four hours or more.

When the train was ready to pull out for Alpena, young Gene was not among the passengers. He had visited the saloon, had been taken in by individuals who apparently made an easy living by fleecing lumberjacks, had become dead drunk and hauled off to a motel room. When he awoke hours later his wallet, watch, and even a ring were gone.

Gene, ashamed to go home broke, caught the next train back to the lumber camp. Again he worked and saved for several months. This time when he started for home, he braced himself to be more leary of the people in Valentine. He vowed to take just one drink. But it didn't work out that way. When he awoke the next morning in a dingy hotel room, he had been "rolled" again.

There was nothing he could do except go back to camp again. A third attempt to go home ended in a similar experience.

It was near Christmas about 1895, when the unyielding urge to go home cropped up in Gene for the fourth time. Again he had saved his earning for several months and was determined not to be taken in this time by the pitfalls of Valentine.

Just west of Valentine about where the railroad tracks curved eastward into the village was a water tank where the trains stopped to replenish their engines with water for steam-making for the return trip to Alpena. Gene was ever-minded of his previous attempts to go home. Just as the train stopped for water a thought popped into his mind. He hurried to the door of the passenger car and jumped out, he traveled north about a half mile, eastward a mile or so and then south until he came to the tracks again. In this way he by-passed Valentine. After waiting in the cold for several hours, he succeeded in flagging down the train and reached home in time for Christmas

NOTE: The Valentine branch of the D & M ended its services about 1904. For all practical purposes Valentine ended at the same time. A few houses and some of the business places remained for a time, but forest fires took their toll within a few years. I can remember the little school house that stood on the hill just to the north of the village proper. It seems that I can remember the old abandoned wooden hotel, but of this I am not sure.

The railroad grades were constructed by hand in those days with round pointed shovels and wheelbarrows. Many of the old D & M grades are evident still. Along the sides of each are numerous holes from which the men shoveled earth on to the roadbed.

As was true with many early lumbering villages, Valentine was built around a large spring which was the main source of water for the villagers.

Chances are the lumbering camp-bosses did not object to having their men waylaid and robbed, for wthout money they were obliged to return to camp and more hard work.

Would it not be wonderful to know someone who attended the Valentine school? Undoubtedly some of these people are living.

Several of us know one person who lived at Valentine. She is Mrs. Nora Secrist, the mother of our present Sheriff Joel Secrist. Mrs. Secrist's father Ed Ewing owned and operated the Valentine Hotel for a few years near the end of its existence. Mrs. Secrist, who then was a young girl, remembers when as many as fifty-two railroad employees ate at the hotel dining room. Is not this fact enough to warrant at least a historical marker at the site of this former city.

Another incident involving Valentine residents is also interesting and amusing. Wilbur Lake operated a barber shop there and later barbered in Atlanta for a long time. He and a friend, Jack Lowe of Valentine, a lumberjack who also lived in Atlanta in later years, perhaps were the first to inaugurate the practice of shining deer.

In those early days people allowed their livestock to run at large. Gardens, field crops and the like were fenced and horses, cows, and hogs roamed over the rest of the land.

It seems that on this occasion Jack and Wilbur were roaming the countryside on foot near Valentine with a crude light hoping to catch the shining eyes of a deer. Shortly a pair of eyes stared right at them. Wilbur held the light and Jack aimed as good as the light would allow and fired. Down went the animal. The men hurried over to see their prize. They had killed a horse.

They pondered a moment and then Jack said, "Well Wilbur I guess we've killed a horse." "We me eye," retorted Wilbur, "It was you who shot it!"

LIFE AT THE SHINGLE MILL, ONE TOSS AND A SUMMER'S WORK GONE - IN EARLY MONTMORENCY COUNTY

By Ross O. Stevens (1967)

Probably every pioneer family had at least one experience that should be recorded for the benefit of future generations. Too many places that now are taken for granted were scenes of great activity in the early days. The George Reed family and the Shingle Mill community near the present Shingle Mill Bridge on the East Branch of the Black River are important components of our early society.

Dora Powell, daughter of one of our earliest pioneer families, the Charles Powells, and George Reed were united in marriage at the Remington home on Spiess Lake (then Remington Lake)* in 1897.

The Reeds established their first home at the Shingle Mill lumbering community in 1898 in a small log cabin near the big boiling spring just north of the present road which leads across the East Branch. Although the cabin was crude, it was made comfortable by filling in spaces between the logs with mud and moss, and by papering the inside with newspapers, a common custom in those days.

A branch of the D. and M. Railroad extended from Valentine along much of what is now Rouse Road, except that it circledthe south side of Rattlesnake Hill and passed directly in front of the Shingle Mill community. Much of the old railroad grade is still visible.

As well as being a woods worker, George Reed was a budding young barber. Since there were not many places to go, not many of the lumberjacks of the camp cared too much how they looked. When they did seek the professional services of Mr. Reed, there was just a big brush heap of hair and six months' growth of beard to mow down, all for twenty-five cents.

To do her part, Mrs. Reed did washing and mending for the lumberjacks. She earned every penny. The average washing came to ten or fifteen cents.

More than once Mrs. Reed walked from their home on the East Branch to Valentine to board the train for Alpena. On one occasion there was no passenger car, so she rode the caboose all the way to Alpena.

The regular bunkhouse did not have room for all who came to work at the shingle mill. The Reeds improvised a bedroom for two of the extras using a common bed sheet to separate the two bedrooms. Hubert Powell, Mrs. Reed's brother, and Lon Valentine were the two that lived and boarded with the Reeds.

One day a terrific thunderstorm ripped through the settlement. Mrs. Reed was cooking the evening meal consisting of bean soup and homemade bread at the time. Store bread was not even dreamed of in those days.

The storm turned into a twister, and in less time than it takes to say "scat," the roof of the Reed cabin was hurled to a vacant spot in the yard. Mrs. Reed could stand it no longer. She dashed out of the house. The first thing she came to was a big pine stump which she clung to for dear life until the storm subsided. When eventually she returned to the remains of her home, the bean soup was still cooking and the bread had finished baking just as though nothing had happened. It was still raining.

With her umbrella for protection, Mrs. Reed walked to the cook camp to see if temporary shelter could be found there. A Mr. and Mrs. Brown were the cooks, but they too were having troubles, so this brave young lady returned to her topless home. By this time the three men had returned from work.

They would make out all right, they decided. With the rain adding a little flavor, the bean soup and bread were eaten as though it were an everyday occurrence. It was a funny sight with the men sitting around the table with their raincoats and hats on and Mrs. Reed perched snugly under her umbrella.

Eventually the rain stopped, but before it did everything was soaked. Soon four brave people tucked themselves into their very wet bunks, and the heavenly breezes bathed their faces all night. The next day the roof was restored to the cabin, and home for the Reeds was complete once more.

Early settlers often traveled long distances in pursuit of entertainment and social activities. The Reeds were no exception. George Reed was an ardent baseball fan and played on the unbeatable Big Rock team. Big Rock at that time was the center of much activity. Quite often after the Saturday evening meal, the Reeds and perhaps some of the younger set at the Shingle Mill community would set out on foot for Big Rock. Someone would carry the lantern and Mr. Reed would take his guitar. Much of the way would be accompanied by songs and guitar playing.

Not only did these activities help break the monotony of walking, walking, walking, but also they helped keep away wild animals. Canadian lynxes, timber wolves, and other wild beasts seemed to enjoy harassing these young people. A common occurrence was for a lynx to let out a blood-curdling cry behind the travelers, and then in a few minutes the same cry would come from in front. Many times these activities would keep up for miles. It was no place for the fainthearted.

The Reed party would follow the railroad grade around the south side of Rattlesnake Hill until they came to Connor's No. 2, which had been a large pine lumbering community. There they would follow a township road that extended southward across the swamp and came out near old Camp 24, and thence to Big Rock.

Generally the party would arrive at Big Rock about sunrise, sleep for a few hours, the men in some farmer's hay mow, and then attend or participate in the ball game. Later they might attend a dance until the wee hours and then start back for their Shingle Mill home. Sometimes a company team and wagon would give them a lift back home.

Times were different back in those days. Pay was meager to begin with, but more often than not the shingle mill owners did not have money to pay the laborers. The workers stayed on hoping things would be better. They knew too that chances were if they went elsewhere the conditions would be the same or even worse. At least at the shingle mill they had been working and were getting fed.

Had it not been for the few quarters Mr. Reed picked up by barbering and a few more dollars Mrs. Reed took in from her efforts, the receipts in terms of money would have been small indeed.

When the summer's work was over and the day of settlement came, all there was to pay the men with were the supplies in the company store. Mr. Reed came a little late and found himself at the end of the line. By the time he arrived at the company store, all had been taken except a few pounds of flour and a large wooden bucket with seven or eight pounds of lard.

Mr. Reed sauntered back to his small cabin, and as gently as possible broke the sad news to his young wife. Tears slowly rolled down her cheeks as she set about melting the lard and transferring it from the large bucket to a small pail for easier and safer carrying.

Already Mr. Reed had loaded all their belongings on the wagon and had hitched the horses.

"Don't forget the lard in the little pail," reminded Mrs. Reed, who already had taken her seat on the wagon. "Bring it here and I can keep it right between my feet."

"Lard? What lard? What pail?" asked Mr. Reed.

"It sets right there by the door," directed Mrs. Reed.

"Oh, my goodness, I thought that was water and threw it out," exclaimed Mr. Reed. "Already I have put the pail in the wagon."

Mrs. Reed wept loudly. "Oh, George," she sighed, "that was our whole summer's work."

Like the good pioneers they were, however, they soon regained their composure and decided to start all over again.

POSTSCRIPT: The daughters of George and Dora Reed, Eulah Marquart and Reba Bean, then of Vanderbilt and Alpena respectively, provided much of the information on which this story is based.

In about 1912 or 1913 my father (George Stevens) made a deal for the lumber in the Shingle Mill buildings. As the bunkhouse was being torn down, a large rattlesnake was found curled in the straw of one of the bunks.

The road south from Connor's No. 2 across the swamp was used to some extent as late as the Model T Ford days. The last time I bumpity-bumped through there with my Model T, the bridge across the little creek had been broken, and for about three feet on one side the auto wheels had just a six-inch plank to carry them across. Right then I decided that if the good Lord would allow me safe passage that time, I would never try it again. I have many unanswered questions about the Shingle Mill establishment. Was the camp built and used during the pine lumbering days or was it built just for the shingle mill operations? I assume the shingles were manufactured from cedar. Also, I don't know whether this branch of the D.& M. Railroad had come and gone before the shingle mill was established or was still in business during the shingle mill operations.

*   *Spiess Lake, as it was called in 1966, is now known as Lake Inez. Its original name was Bargehr Lake, named after the family that homesteaded on its shores.*

ALL MIXED UP OVER A WOMAN IN EARLY MONTMORENCY COUNTY

By Ross O. Stevens (1967)

This story was told to me by Raymond Willyard of Johannesburg. Ever since we bought the old Willyard homestead in Section 4 of Vienna Township, about two miles east of Hetherton, I have wanted to meet Mr. Willyard. What do you know? We are roommate patients in Gaylord Memorial Hospital, and just as I had suspected, Ray knows much about early Montmorency County history. He was born in 1890 on the old homestead. Our story is not too important, but it does show a little part of the lighter side of life in those old days. Camp 24 on the Boyne City, Gaylord, and Alpena railroad was nicely getting under way. The year was about 1913. Chris Bloomfield had bought a new wood cook stove from the company store at Camp 24 and with the help of the store clerk had strapped it over his shoulders and was carrying it to his shack about four miles northwest of Camp 24.

Although the stove weighed more than 100 pounds it was not too much of a load for Chris, for he was a huge man, unmarried, in his middle thirties. Although he had much strength he seldom used it for good purposes. He preferred rather to trap and hunt and fish and pick wild berries for a living. Generally he was very grizzled and his clothing was roughly patched as only a man would patch them. The shack he lived in was one that had been left behind by a lumber company many years before.

It was shortly after noon on a winter day that Chris plodded towards home with his heavy load. About half the way was along a well used log road. The rest was along a foot path not so often used. While walking along the log road Chris met a young Indian and his wife riding on a set of sleighs and headed for Camp 24. The Indian was a saw filer by trade and had been hired by the White Lumber Company.

As was very much the custom in those days, the Indian couple and Chris stopped to pass the time of day and chat a bit. Almost immediately Chris was smitten by the beauty of the young Indian woman and did every thing he could to prolong the visit. He would shift his load from one shoulder to the other and think up new things to talk about. His talk was directly mostly to the man but his glances mostly were toward the young woman.

The horses pulling the sleigh became cold and fidgety, but Chris talked on. It was evident the young man and his wife wanted to travel on, but not Chris. He had never seen anyone as beautiful as the young Indian lady.

Finally the young Indian man spoke to his horses and they started off on a trot. Nearly two hours had passed. As the horses pulled away Chris allowed that he needed a rest and removed the heavy stove from his shoulder.

Whew, he thought, why didn't I think of resting my back before. "That woman," he mumbled.

During the long visit on the road the Indian couple had asked Chris to come to Camp 24 and visit them. He did so, and without much delay.

At first the visits were two or three weeks apart but before long had become almost weekly and always just in time for the evening meal. As time passed it became evident that Chris was more interested in the Indian's wife than in the man. Naturally the Indian did not like this situation.

Winter faded into spring and Chris still felt compelled to make the journey to the Indians' cabin located on the outskirts of the camp. Finally one evening a mild discussion took place between the Indian, his wife and Chris. When the wife entered the argument on the side of Chris, the Indian jumped up, put on his hat and coat and stalked out of the house obviously disturbed.

Shortly thereafter at the urging on the Indian woman, Chris picked up his 30-30 rifle which he practically always carried both day and night and headed homeward. Not more than a quarter of a mile down the past a huge manly figure appeared in the dim moonlight not more than thirty feet away.

Immediately Chris thought about the Indian. "Hello" he said as he squared himself in the path. There was no reply.

"Hello there, I say, answer me," Chris snorted. Still no reply came forth, but instead two arms seemed to rise in the darkness.

"Now listen," continued Chris. "Either you say hello or I'll shoot, I'm not fooling."

Another step or two nearer it came and the 30-30 barked loudly. It was a big bear that fell dead almost at Chris' feet. For a week or two this incident stopped all nightly excursions by Chris, but before long he mustered enough courage to again stop by the Indians' residence.

In the meantime the Indian had warned his wife that unless Chris Bloomfield stayed away from their home he would shoot him. To show that he meant it the Indian put a shell in his single barrel shot gun and placed it where it would be handy.

Chris knew that frequently the Indian worked late on Thursday evenings and he chose this day of the week for his next visit. Even though the Indian's wife explained her husband's anger and determination to end the affair, Chris seemed in no hurry to leave. But earlier than usual footsteps were heard coming towards the front of the house.

"Hurry, run out the back door before you get shot," urged the woman, and with that Chris beat it as fast as his big frame would allow.

The Indian caught sight of the fleeing man, dashed for the gun, ran to the back door and blasted away.

Some of the boys at the camp had told Chris of the Indian's plans to shoot. While the Indian's wife was in the kitchen, Chris had dropped a bottle cork into the gun barrel. The only result of the Indian's gun blast was to blow the end of the gun barrel off.

Chris took the hint, however, and never visited the Indian family again.

ACKNOWLEDGEMENTS

It would be impossible for me to remember all who contributed in some way to the publication of this collection of stories. To those I have neglected to mention here, I apologize for the omission, but am appreciative of them no less.

First, I thank Sarah, my wife, for not only her patience with my time spent over the years on the Can't Hardly stories, but for her suggestions and editing help as each developed.

As many know, these tales were first published in the Montmorency County Tribune over a period of nearly ten years, beginning in 2005. I am very grateful to the Tribune editors and publishers during those years, Tom Young, Jim Young, and Bill and Michelle Pinson, for providing the initial forum for the Can't Hardly tales. (The Tribune also published the stories written by Dad in 1966 and 1967. John Weber was the publisher and editor then.)

I also, of course, thank the various contributors for the stories included in Part II of this book and the additional tales they provided for the Can't Hardly column in the Tribune. Other writers were Ernie Paul and Barry Danks.

Then there were the many who helped me reconstruct memories of the decades old events which are depicted in my stories. My partners in the Can't Hardly Lumber Company activities, Larry Wilson, Darrell Briley and Bob Teets, helped not only with those stories, but others as well. Mary Ann Marlatt, Karen Friday, Robin McMurphy, Oral McMurphy, Vernon Klein, David Manier, Rod Marlatt, Terry Brooks, Dennis

Briley, Patsy Brooks, Joyce Ehrlick (my sister), Claudia Sherwood, Maurice Carey, Jim Smith and others (beyond my immediate recall) provided many of the details included in my stories.

I also thank Julie Mowery and Kathy Grow for technical assistance in producing the stories over the years. I also acknowledge the role my former wife, Karen Stevens, a lifelong, accomplished English teacher and writer, had with my early writing endeavors which led ultimately to these tales.

Finally, I thank the editor of my stories for this book, Karen Kingsley, for her outstanding work that improved the readability of the stories across the board.